# Personal Soulwinning

A Handbook on Winning the Lost

# Personal Soulwinning

A Handbook on Winning the Lost

Including 175 Soulwinning Tips

by
Frank R. Shivers

Unless otherwise noted, Scripture quotations are from
The Holy Bible *King James Version*

Library of Congress Cataloging-in-Publication Data

Shivers, Frank R., 1949-
Personal Soulwinning / Frank Shivers
ISBN 978-1-878127-53-2


Library of Congress Control Number:
2023913995

Cover design by
Tim King


For Information:
Frank Shivers Evangelistic Association
2005 Congress Road
Hopkins, South Carolina 29061
www.frankshivers.com

PRESENTED TO

_____

BY

_____

DATE

_____

# Publications by the author to help the soulwinner

*The Evangelism Apologetic Study Bible*

*Soulwinning 101*

*Evangelistic Praying*

*Evangelistic Preaching 101*

*Christian Basics 101* (Follow-up resource)

*Growing in Knowledge, Living by Faith*
(Follow-up resource)

*The Evangelistic Invitation 101*

*Spurs to Soul Winning* (365 Daily Challenges)

*Revivals 101*

*Persecuted for Christ*

*Personal Soulwinning*

*False Hopes of Heaven* (Tract booklet)

*The Death Clock* (Tract Booklet)

*The Goal Line Stand* (Tract Booklet)

*First Steps for the New Believer* (Tract booklet)

To

Steve Roberts

A loyal friend, prayer warrior, faithful pastor, and fervent soulwinner.

# Contents

"If God shall bless us to the winning of souls, our work shall remain when the wood and hay and stubble of earth's art and science shall have gone to the dust from which they sprang. In Heaven itself the soulwinner, blessed of God, shall have memorials of his work preserved forever in the galleries of the skies."[1]

~C. H. Spurgeon

# Preface

*Personal Soulwinning* was birthed while preparing to preach upon this subject at Community Bible Church, Beaufort, South Carolina.

This book based on New Testament principles and requirements of soulwinning, nearly sixty years of the author's practice and insights from history's greatest soulwinners (evangelists, pastors, and Evangelism Professors), is written to prompt, encourage, and equip the reader to win their first soul to Christ (or enhance their ability to win more), provide a handbook for the experienced soulwinner to train others in the work and furnish a soulwinning textbook for Evangelism classes in Christian schools, colleges, and seminaries.

In this book, the reader will learn how to overcome the fear of soulwinning, jumpstart gospel conversations, make gospel presentations, develop soulwinning methods, debunk hampering excuses for postponing salvation, utilize a soulwinning marked New Testament, disciple new believers, and call for decisions (draw the net). Included are 175 tips for the soulwinner.

No work stands nearer to the Savior's heart or is counted as critical as personal soulwinning. He authorized it. He practiced it. He commanded it. It's time you and I do it. Spurgeon, speaking to believers, said, "Your one business in life is to lead men to believe in Jesus Christ by the power of the Holy Spirit, and every other thing should be made subservient to this one objective."[2]

Throw out the lifeline of salvation (for the first or hundredth time) without delay to save a soul that's gone astray.

> Soon will the season of rescue be o'er;
> Soon will they drift to eternity's shore.
> Haste then, my brother, no time for delay,
> But throw out the lifeline and save them today!
> ~Edward S. Ufford (1888)

"Make the most of your chances to tell others the Good News. Be wise in all your contacts with them" (Colossians 4:5 TLB).

Rescue the perishing;
Care for the dying;
      Snatch them in pity from sin and the grave.
Weep o'er the erring one;
Lift up the fallen;
      Tell them of Jesus, the mighty to save.

                      ~Fanny Crosby (1869)

# 1
## The Soulwinners' Work

As he neared the sunset of life, Lyman Beecher was asked what he counted to be the most important thing. Without hesitation, he replied, "It is not theology; it is not controversy; *it is saving souls.*" He was referring to soul-winning.

What is soulwinning? Soulwinning is the distraught shepherd who leaves the ninety-and-nine, endangering his life, to search out and find the one lost sheep to bring it back to the fold (Luke 15:4–5). It is the despairing woman who diligently and relentlessly searches for the *one* lost coin until it is found and safely is in her hand (Luke 15:8–9). It is the concerned father who patiently and lovingly searches for the *one* lost son in the far country until he is rescued and safely at home (Luke 15:11–24). Soulwinning is every Christian's job. C. H. Spurgeon said, "Soul-winning is the chief business of the Christian minister; it should be the main pursuit of every true believer."[3]

A working definition of soulwinnng is offered by John R. Rice. "By saving souls, we do not mean getting people to join the church, to be reformed, or to go through certain religious rites. To be a soulwinner is to cause people to realize their need for Christ as their personal Savior and to lead them to commit themselves wholly to Him with heart faith."[4] Soulwinning is fishing for (Luke 5:10) and catching—bringing to faith in Christ (Acts 5:14)—lost (Luke 19:10), blinded (Ephesians 4:18), captive (Luke 4:18), dead (Ephesians 2:1), and condemned (John 3:18) souls through the power of the Holy Spirit (Acts 1:8). Soulwinning is rescue work, the throwing out of the life buoy of salvation to perishing souls sinking ever downward toward an eternity in Hell (Colossians 1:13).

*The soulwinner is one who is sent.* He is Divinely tasked with sharing the Gospel with lost man at large. Additionally, when God convicts a sinner, He commissions a saint to go to him with the Word of salvation. W. B. Riley asserts, "The same God who convicted Saul commissioned Ananias. I sometimes wonder if there is ever a convicted man without another commissioned at the same moment. I doubt seriously if God ever brings a man under condemnation for sin without saying to someone of the saints, 'Go to that man!'"[5] When the Ethiopian eunuch was brought under the Holy Spirit's conviction, God said to Philip, "Go near, and join thyself to this chariot" (Acts 8:29).

*The soulwinner goes to whom he is sent.* The soulwinner sows the gospel seed beside all waters (Isaiah 32:20). He cannot be choosy. Spurgeon said, "The text [Matthew 18:12] warns us that we are not to despise one person, even because of evil character. The first temptation is to despise one because he is the only one. The next is to despise one because that one is so little. The next and perhaps the most dangerous form of the temptation is to despise one because that one has gone astray. The individual is not on the right path. He is not obeying the Law nor reflecting credit on the church but doing much that vexes the spiritual and grieves the holy. But we are not, therefore, to despise him. Read the eleventh verse: 'The Son of man is come to save that which was lost.'"[6]

All must be told the Good News—"the small and the great"—without regard to face, race, or lifestyle. E. Y. Mullins said, "If the soulwinner is governed by external appearances, if he thinks more of the social level or the immoral character or the degree of ignorance of those he seeks to win, he will make little headway. The genuine soulwinner sees beneath the surface and knows that the power of Jesus Christ is capable of going down into the very springs of human conduct. He believes that Christ can uncover hidden possibilities and that redeeming grace can transform into the divine image the most repulsive of human beings."[7]

*The soulwinner goes where he is sent.*

1. Like Jesus. Jesus won souls at a cemetery. He won a soul up in a tree. He won two souls on a lake as they fished. He won a woman at a well. He won Paul on the Damascus Road. He won Andrew at a house. He won a man on a crowded street. He won the thief on the Cross. Develop a mindset to look for opportunities everywhere, even in the least preferable places, to introduce people to Christ. One of the oddest places where I won a soul was in a hog

pen (fenced-in, boggy, stinking field) while in a revival meeting in Conway, South Carolina.

2. Like Paul. Paul witnessed in the synagogue, aboard ships, in prison, house to house, and in the household of Caesar. Like Paul, we must look upon every person as a soul for whom Jesus provided salvation by His death, and every place as a potential soul-saving station (home, hospital, nursing home, farm, church, business, sports arena, rescue mission, school campus, deepest jungle in Africa).

3. Like D. L. Moody. Moody said, "Every place where God leads, there is your field." Moody won the souls of the poorest children on the streets of Chicago, soldiers in Grant's army, troops in Confederate prison camps, and the wounded in army field hospitals. One writer gave this account of Moody's evangelistic efforts: "It is said that in holding special meetings for the conversion of his fellowmen, Mr. Moody has traveled over 1,000,000 miles, has addressed over 100,000,000 persons—25 million of whom were young people—and *has dealt personally* with nearly 750,000 individuals."[8]

4. Like Frank Jenner. For 28 years from his conversion, until Parkinson's disease prevented him, Jenner aimed to talk to ten people daily about Christ (usually on George Street in Sydney, Australia).[9] He probably spoke of Christ to more than 100,000 people in total.[10]

*The soulwinner goes when he is sent.* The soulwinner promptly and resolutely responds to the Spirit's prompting to witness, despite the cost, when summoned. To delay may result in a soul's eternal damnation. The door of opportunity open today may be closed tomorrow. Spurgeon remarked, "Do not give place to the Devil by delay! Haste while opportunity and quickening are in happy conjunction. Do not be caught in your nets, but break the meshes of worldliness and away where glory calls you."[11]

Note that God always has the right to interrupt the believer's schedule without notice, having him forgo the big game, cut class, miss work, or skip a meal to make a witness. Be His minuteman, ready to stop everything to go when beckoned, without balking or excuses. In England, a man was to be hung. His mother interceded on his behalf before the king and prevailed in getting a pardon. The page commissioned to deliver the pardon stopped to watch a clown performing and then hurried to fulfill his errand. He arrived minutes too late. While giving account to the king, he said, "I laughed with the crowd at the clown, and the time slipped away." Many Christians laugh at the clown and enjoy life and its pleasures as time slips away and souls die without Jesus.

The Christian should engage in soulwinning in response to seven calls.

*The Call from the Bible.* General Booth said, "Put your ear down to the Bible and hear Him bid you go and pull sinners out of the fire of sin." Scripture says, "Ye shall be witnesses unto me both in Jerusalem [home area], and in all Judaea [state], and in Samaria [across America], and unto the uttermost part of the earth [everywhere else]" (Acts 1:8); "I have chosen you,…that ye should go and bring forth fruit" (John 15:16); "Follow me, and I will make you fishers of men" (Matthew 4:19); and "Go ye into all the world, and preach the gospel to every creature" (Mark 16:15). The instruction is not a good suggestion; it's an imperative order. As Hudson Taylor said, "The Great Commission is not an option to be considered; it is a command to be obeyed."

*The Call from the Lost.* Broken lives from Hill to Dell cry for meaning and purpose in life (Luke 4:18). Helen Smith Shoemaker wrote, "People are lost and need to be found. They search for God, ultimate reality, and faith, but they cannot find the most important door in the world, which is the door through which people walk when they find God."[12] The lost cry out for us to show them that door (John 10:9). Spurgeon asserts, "Men are either going to Heaven or to Hell—and it is time that we came to close grips with them about this all-important matter!"

*The Call from the Example of New Testament Believers.* Andrew won Simon Peter (John 1:40–42). Phillip witnessed to Nathaniel and brought him to Jesus (John 1:45–46). Paul won Onesimus (Philemon 10), and Silas teamed up with him to win the Philippi jailer (Acts 16:28–31). John the Baptist won two disciples to Christ (John 1:35–

39). The soulwinning example of these and others in the New Testament exhort us to walk in their steps.

*The Call from the Example of Jesus.* Jesus' ministry commenced with the winning of Andrew (John 1:40) and ended with the winning of the penitent thief on the Cross (Luke 23:43). The New Testament records at least nineteen soulwinning encounters of our Lord. His example of winning lost souls implores imitation. When He ascended to Heaven, He passed the witnessing baton to His children (Acts 1:8).

*The Call from the Tormented in Hell.* From the pits of Hell, the call rings loudly to win souls. The rich man in Hell pleaded that someone would be sent to warn his five brothers lest they end up in Hell with him (Luke 16:27–28). Similar cries still ascend to the redeemed from that place of eternal torment.

*The Call from the Transformed Heart.* W. A. Criswell said, "The first impulse of a born-again Christian is to win somebody to Jesus."[13] C. E. Matthews says, "The best evidence of an individual's regeneration is that he tries to win the lost to Christ."[14] Like Paul, the believer testifies, "I am made all things to all men, that I might by all means save some" (1 Corinthians 9:22). A blind man's eyesight was restored by the hands of a skilled medical missionary. The man disappeared for a few days and returned to the missionary's home. When he opened the door, the missionary was stunned to see the man holding one end of a rope that ten blind men clutched. When blinded eyes are opened to the truth about salvation, they find a rope and bring all the blind they can to Him, who makes them see.

*The Call from the Spiritual Giants of the Faith.* What John Wesley said to preachers applies to all: "You have nothing to do but to win souls. Therefore, spend and be spent in the work. It's not your business to preach so many times but to save as many souls as you can." John R. Rice said, "Do you love Christ? If so, then you will win souls. If you make a small effort to win souls, then your love is small. If you make none, then how can you say you love Him at all?" George W. Truett said, "If one is born again, that one is concerned that somebody else may be saved." General Booth said, "'Not called!' did you say? 'Not heard the call,' I think you should say." L. R. Scarborough said, "Every Christian is called in the hour of salvation to witness a winning testimony for Jesus Christ. Nothing in Heaven or earth can excuse him from it. God gives no furloughs from this heaven-born obligation." Lewis Drummond said, "A proper theology of evangelism…will result in a profound zeal to win the lost."[15] Andrew Murray said, "We sometimes hesitate to speak of men being converted and saved by men. Let us not hesitate to accept it as part of our work, of our high prerogative as the sons of God, to convert and to save men [James 5:20]."[16]

Spurgeon forthrightly stated, "Pardoned sinners, possessed of the Holy Spirit, rejoicing in salvation and upheld in the consistency of life, are the chosen instruments of God for the conversion of their fellowmen. I see…nothing in the Scriptures about a certain class of officials being set apart to convert sinners to the exclusion of others."[17] A. T. Pierson said, "To neglect souls is treachery to our trust and treason to our Lord." Jonathan Edwards stated, "Do we who have the care of souls know what Hell is? Have we seen the state of the damned? Are we aware of how dreadful their case is? Do we know that most people go there unaware of their danger? And do we see that our hearers are not aware of their danger? If we knew all this, it would be morally impossible for us to avoid passionately telling them the dreadfulness of that misery and their great exposure to it. We would cry aloud to them."[18]

This seven-fold call to soulwinning demands we find a way, make a way, and use it, even if it's unconventional and criticized, to get the Gospel to the lost multitudes. Christians must become 'all things to all men so that by all possible means, *they* might win some' (1 Corinthians 9:22 NIV).

> They will not seek; they must be sought.
> They will not come; they must be brought.
> They will not study; they must be taught.
>
> ~ Unknown

Soulwinning is important for five reasons:

1. Soulwinning helps the believer. Murray Downey states, "Soulwinning helps the Christian live right."[19] Bill Bright says,

"Witnessing will stimulate your spiritual growth, lead you to pray and study God's Word, and encourage you to depend on Christ."[20]

2. Soulwinning helps the world. Soulwinning is the only cure for a sick and depraved world. Neither government nor religion is able to make the world better. Christ is the world's only hope. Robert Louis Stevenson talked about his fascination with the gas lamplighter as a child. He stated that as the lamplighter lit the lamps in his community, he would rush to his mother, exclaiming, "Come see a man who is punching holes in the darkness." Soulwinning punches holes in the spiritual darkness that envelops the world.

3. Soulwinning helps the sinner. It enables the unsaved (the spiritually blinded) to find abundant, eternal life in Christ (John 10:10). "To open their eyes, that they may be converted from darkness to light, and from the power of Satan to God, that they may receive forgiveness of sins, and a lot among the saints, by the faith that is in me" (Acts 26:18 DRA). Soulwinners, not angelic messengers, are God's ordained method of reaching the world. Horatius Bonar said, "The soul and eternity of one man depend upon the voice of another!" Spurgeon asserts, "The Gospel will not be revealed to men by any supernatural agency; we must go with it. They cannot learn it without being taught it. No man will know the Gospel unless somebody shall tell it to him by word of mouth, or by the gift of a book or a tract, or by a letter, or by the open preaching of the Word."[21]

4. Soulwinning helps the church. Soulwinning produces spiritual muscle in the body of Christ and its work. It increases baptisms, workers, and tithers to the church. It adds new members to the church and builds the Sunday school. It expands the missionary program of the church. It prevents church decay, stagnation, and death. It promotes unity among the brethren. (People who witness together love one another.) Someone has said, "The cure of a sick church is to put it on a soulwinning diet."

5. Soulwinning helps honor Christ. Spurgeon said, "But the best argument of all [for evangelism] is to be found in the wounds of Jesus. You want to honor Him, you desire to put many crowns upon His head, and you can best do this by winning souls for Him. These

are the spoils that He covets; these are the trophies for which He fights; these are the jewels that shall be His best adornment."

# 2

# The Soulwinners' Message

"Go ye into all the world, and preach the gospel to every creature" (Mark 16:15). What is the Gospel?

*The Gospel is divine good news.* It is the good news of God's intervention in man's deplorable, depraved, and damned estate, providing him a means of deliverance (salvation) from sin's mastery and penalty through God's Son, Jesus Christ. Salvation is all God's work from start to finish. God ordained it. He orchestrated it. He offered it. He oversees it.

*The Gospel is delightful good news.* What makes it such elating good news? It provides forgiveness of sins and reconciliation with God. It provides access to God. It provides an escape from Hell and an eternal Home in Heaven. It delivers from the captivity of sin. It grants hope beyond the veil of death. It provides a peace that passes all understanding in trial and calamity. It delivers from the misery of a sinful, bruised, and crushed life.

*The Gospel is dangerous good news.* All who embrace it are told to "endure hardness, as a good soldier of Jesus Christ" (2 Timothy 2:3). Of the early saints, the author of Hebrews says, "They were stoned to death, they were cut in two, and they died by being murdered with swords. They went around wearing the skins of sheep and goats, needy, oppressed, and mistreated" (Hebrews 11:37 CEB). Jesus forewarned, "The servant is not greater than his lord. If they have persecuted me, they will also persecute you" (John 15:20). Spurgeon poses a frank and all-important question to the believer: "Are you not willing to pass through every ordeal if by any means you may save some? If this be not your spirit, you had better keep to your farm and to your merchandise, for no man will ever win a soul who is not prepared to suffer everything within the compass of possibility for that soul's sake."[22]

*The Gospel is dispersible good news.* "Ye shall be witnesses unto me" (Acts 1:8). The Gospel is not to be hoarded but shared with the whole world.

*The Gospel is dependable good news.* It will do precisely what it advocates, promises, and proclaims (Mark 13:31). It will never disappoint.

*The Gospel is durable good news.* It is unshakeable, unchangeable (Hebrews 12:27). 1) Neither Satan, nor anything else, can undo that which Christ wrought in a man's heart. The person who is born-again is never unborn (John 10:28). 2) The Gospel is so powerful that nothing can interfere with its transformation of sinners until the age of grace comes to an end at the coming of the Lord (Romans 8:29). In light of these six facts, it's understandable why the Gospel is called Good News.

Paul says of the Gospel, "It is the power of God unto salvation to every one that believeth" (Romans 1:16). Christ is the power of God to forgive sin and reconcile the soul to Himself. "The weapon with which the Lord conquers men is the truth as it is in Jesus."[23] He is the soulwinner's message—the simple, singular truth of His redemptive work to save sinners through His atoning death and victorious resurrection (1 Corinthians 15:1–4).

"The soulwinner's message," asserts Paul Little, "includes and revolves around five truths: 1) Jesus Christ, who He is; 2) Jesus' diagnosis of human nature; 3) the fact and meaning of the crucifixion of Jesus Christ; 4) the fact and meaning of the resurrection of Jesus Christ; and 5) the *how* of becoming a Christian."[24]

Spurgeon says, "The great truth is the cross, the truth that 'God so loved the world that he gave his only begotten son that whosoever believeth in him should not perish but have everlasting life.' Brethren, keep to that. That is the bell for you to ring. Ring it, man! Ring it! Keep on ringing it."[25] Scarborough wrote, "The winner needs to be right on the plan of salvation. This is basic. Salvation is by grace through faith plus nothing."[26]

Tell the world of saving grace;
Make it known in ev'ry place.
    Ring it out; ring it out.
Help the needy ones to know
Him from whom all blessings flow.
    Ring it out; ring it out.

~ James Rowe (1911)

### The Gospel in a Verse: John 14:6

"I am the way, the truth, and the life: no man cometh unto the Father, but by me" (John 14:6). Jesus is the *Way* man is reconciled to God (John 14:6a). "For there is one God, and one mediator between God and men, the man Christ Jesus" (1 Timothy 2:5). In Christ, the sinner is pardoned of sin and granted access into the presence of God. Christ is not one of many ways to reconcile with God (salvation), but man's only way. "No one comes to the Father, but by me" (John 14:6 RSV).

Jesus is the *truth*, the embodiment of all that is true and excellent (John 14:6b). "Thy word is truth" (John 17:17). His promises are sure and dependable. As Truth, Christ reveals light to the darkness and depravity in man's soul. He contradicts falsehood and reveals deception.

Jesus is the *life,* the source of abundant and eternal life (John 14:6c; John 10:10). Christ is man's Paraclete, comforter, and helper who makes life meaningful, bearable, and happy. Christ is "the resurrection and the life," raising those that die to newness of life (John 11:25) to dwell with Him and saved loved ones eternally in Heaven (John 14:2–3).

### The Gospel in a Verse: John 3:16

"For God so loved the world, that he gave his only begotten Son, that whosoever believeth in him should not perish, but have everlasting life" (John 3:16).

*The great subject of salvation.* "Not perish." God's offer of salvation aims to forgive man of sin and release him from its destructive penalty. No matter is of greater importance than that of getting right with God.

*The great stimulus of salvation.* "For God so loved." God's incomprehensible, immeasurable, and unspeakable love prompted the sacrifice of His Son for man's sin so that we might be saved. Henry Ward Beecher said, "The life and death of Christ was but the working out of the love of God. The affection and the yearning of heart towards His erring creatures were just the same in God before Christ came that Christ showed it to be while He was on earth. It is just the same still. There is no change in God or His love."[27]

*The great source of salvation.* "Only begotten Son." Jesus is God's unique Son who left Heaven to come to earth "to seek and to save that which was lost." He lived sinlessly and died vicariously at Calvary to redeem man from sin. Salvation is only available in and through a personal relationship with Him (Acts 4:12).

*The great scope of salvation.* "Whosoever." Spurgeon says, "From the moralist to the utterly vile, from the grey-headed sinner to the boy or maiden." All may come who will come. I am thankful that the text reads "whosoever," for had it used the name Frank Shivers, I would not know if it meant me or another named the same.

*The great summons of salvation.* "Believeth." Salvation is not automatic. It must be received. The word *believeth* denotes an invitation to gain it by faith. Although salvation is available to all people, it avails only for those who take it by faith and repentance. President Andrew Jackson offered a pardon to George Wilson, who had been sentenced to death. The man refused the amnesty. Supreme Court Justice John Marshall declared, "The value of the pardon depends upon its acceptance. If it is refused, then there is no pardon." Mr. Mitchell died on the gallows. Even so, God's offer of pardon must be accepted to be granted.

*The great surety of salvation.* "Should not perish, but have everlasting life." The good news to him that is perishing in his sins is that God has provided the means to avert that form of life and death. No man must die lost, estranged from God in sin, and enter eternal Hell. In Christ, man is promised abundant life presently and eternal life in Heaven (John 10:9–10).

The Gospel in a Short Text: Titus 3:4–8

"That being justified by his grace, we should be made heirs according to the hope of eternal life" (Titus 3:7). Paul sets forth the full scope of salvation in Titus 3:4–8.

*Man's problem before God* (sin). Paul says, "All have sinned, and come short of the glory of God" (Romans 3:23). Man's sin is manifest in attitude and action ("foolish, disobedient, led astray, enslaved to various desires and pleasures, spending our lives in wickedness and envy, despicable, hating one another," Titus 3:3 LEB). The psalmist states, "None is righteous, no, not one" (Romans 3:10 ESV).

*Man's plight without God* (separation). Paul says, "The wages [consequences, penalty] of sin is death" (Romans 6:23). Man, apart from God's intervention, is doomed for a ruinous life presently and destruction in eternity.

*Man's provision from God* (Savior). "But then the kindness and love of God our Savior was made known" (Titus 3:4 ERV). The remedy to the sin problem is the shed blood of Jesus at Calvary (Titus 3:4–7). "Jesus paid it all; all to Him I owe. Sin had left a crimson stain; He washed it white as snow." Jeremiah asks a rhetorical question applicable to the sinner. "Can the Ethiopian change his skin, or the leopard his spots?" (Jeremiah 13:23). See Ephesians 2:8–9. Jonathan Edwards said, "You contribute nothing to your salvation except the sin that made it necessary."

The mighty gulf caused by sin between God and man can only be bridged through a personal relationship with Jesus (1 Timothy 2:5). "This salvation includes justification by His grace, adoption into His family by His love, regeneration by the power of the Holy Ghost, the blessed hope of eternal life while here, and the blessed reality of eternal life hereafter."[28]

*Man's position in God* (sons). Upon justification (forgiveness, mercy, grace), a transformational change takes place. Instantly, we become sons of God (John 1:12; Romans 5:1; 2 Corinthians 5:17). Let us, therefore, talk and walk like children of the King. A sculptor in southern Georgia was asked about the secret behind his carving of beautiful dogs. He thought momentarily and replied, "I whittle off everything that doesn't look like a dog, and it comes out like this." To live worthy of our position as sons of God, we must whittle off everything in our life that doesn't look like a Christian.

*Man's part with God* (service). Paul says, "They which have believed in God might be careful to maintain good works" (Titus 3:8). Good works don't enter the picture of salvation until after the fact (compare Titus 3:5 to Titus 3:8). Spurgeon said, "Not that our salvation should be the effect of our work, but our work should be the evidence of our salvation." A factory worker busy at work was asked by a visitor, "How many people work here?" He replied, "About half of them." That ought never to be true about the church and its members. Paul says, "For we are His workmanship, created in Christ Jesus unto good works" (Ephesians 2:10). No more excellent work can the believer do than to tell another of Christ's gift of salvation (John 4:29).

The Gospel in a Verse: John 3:3

"Ye must be born again" (John 3:7). That which Jesus said to the Jewish rabbi Nicodemus, He says to all—you must be born again. The new birth is not the outward experience of baptism, reformation, alteration of life, church membership, morality, or mere profession of the faith. Billy Graham asserts that the new birth is "the infusing of divine life into the human soul…the implantation or impartation of divine nature into the human soul." It is entering into a right relationship with God through repentance of sin and faith placed in the Lord Jesus Christ. It is a new life complete with a new Ruler, rules, rights, relationships, and resolves (2 Corinthians 5:17). Graham was right to say, "Man can come to Christ by faith and emerge a new man. This sounds incredible—even impossible—yet it is precisely what the Bible teaches."

When Zacchaeus met Jesus in the sycamore tree, he was greedy—and Christ changed him. When John Bunyan came to Christ, he was profane and dishonest—and Christ changed him. When Lee Strobel came to Christ, he was an agnostic—and Christ changed him into an apologist for the Christian faith. When Paul came to Christ on the Damascus Road, he was self-righteous and a persecutor of Christians—and Christ changed him into a preacher of the faith he once denounced. And when Nicodemus met Christ on that Syrian rooftop that night long ago, Christ changed him. These and all the born-again ones say with Rufus McDaniel, "What a wonderful change in my life has been wrought since Jesus came into my heart! I have light in my soul for which long I have sought since Jesus came into my heart!" The new birth—man's sin necessitates it; Calvary provided it; Christ promises it; Christians testify to it; All are invited to experience it.

The Gospel in a Verse: Acts 16:31

"What must I do to be saved?" is the cry of a lost world, and the soulwinner must rightly give an answer. And what is the only correct answer? It's "Believe on the Lord Jesus Christ, and thou shalt be saved" (Acts 16:31). What does it mean for the sinner to believe? When a sinner believes in Christ in the saving sense, he does more than believe in Christ's deity, atoning death for man's sin, resurrection, authority and power to save, and readiness to save. "He believes," Faris Whitesell asserts, "to the extent of thrusting himself wholeheartedly on Christ for time and eternity, of appropriating Christ and all that He has done as his only hope, of turning his whole life Christward for all time. This involves repentance, self-denial, trust, committal, confession, and loyalty."[29] Echoing the same, W. A. Criswell says, "The response, 'believe,' involved turning to Christ. A necessary action for true belief in Christ is repentance, for Jesus said, 'No; but, unless you repent, you will all likewise perish' (Luke 13:3). Repentance and belief are, therefore, two sides of the same coin."[30]

"The more of God's ways we proclaim [God's way of punishing sin, God's way of forgiving sin, God's way of mercy through a sacrifice, God's way of pardon through faith in Jesus]," asserts Spurgeon, "the more likely is it that sinners will be converted unto God."[31]

14

# 3

# The Soulwinners' Equipment

As equipment is necessary for doctors, dentists, lawyers, and carpenters for their trade, it is equally essential for soulwinners to win souls. The soulwinners' equipment is both material and spiritual.

1. A Life Saved by God's Amazing Grace.

Scarborough said, "He must have looked at Christ through eyes of repentance and faith and accepted him as Lord and Master. He must know the way over which he would lead others."[32] Jesus said, 'The blind cannot lead the blind' (Luke 6:39). Spurgeon states, "If you are doubtful as to whether you are saved or not, the sword of the Spirit in your hand is rusted or hidden in a scabbard. You cannot wield the weapons of your holy war with any force while your arm is trembling with doubt. You must know in yourself that you are forgiven and that you have proved the power of the precious blood before you can speak to others with the hope that they will believe your message."[33] See 2 Corinthians 13:5.

2. Dedication.

"Follow me, and I will make you fishers of men" (Matthew 4:19). "We must live Christ," said John Walcot, "if we would successfully speak of Christ. We cannot win souls from death unless we possess Christ's life power, and we cannot be enriched with that power unless we maintain faith in Him and fellowship with Him. If we go forth in this great work, weeping in tears of sympathy for souls and strong in the faith and love of Christ, we shall not labor in vain or spend our strength for naught."

a. Surrender. "I beseech you therefore, brethren, by the mercies of God, that ye present your bodies a living sacrifice, holy, acceptable unto God, which is your reasonable service" (Romans 12:1). Oswald J. Smith says, "If God is going to use us for His honor and glory, if His power is going to rest upon us, if He is going to bless our soulwinning ministry, then our lives must be placed absolutely at His disposal."

b. Separation. Worldly men are not suitable vessels for the Lord's work. To *make* a difference, the Christian must first *be* different. "Wherefore come out from among them, and be ye separate, saith the Lord" (2 Corinthians 6:17). "Let the separation between you and the world," saith Spurgeon, "be final and irreversible. Say, 'Here I go for Christ and His Cross, for the faith of the Bible, for the laws of God, for holiness, for trust in Jesus; and never will I go back, come what may.'"[34]

c. Purity. "Be ye clean, that bear the vessels of the LORD" (Isaiah 52:11). Praying Hyde asserts, "Holiness precedes soulwinning." Spurgeon asserts, "Let a man become holy, and even if he only has the slightest ability, he will be a more fit instrument in God's hand than the man of great acquired skills who is not obedient to divine will nor clean and pure in the sight of the Lord God Almighty."[35]

An employee who worked for a city located in a valley was fired. He angrily plugged the primary pipe that supplied water to the city from the reservoir high in the mountain. Not until he confessed the deed and the line was unplugged did the flow of water resume.

Why no soulwinning desire, power, or fruit? The Spirit's power pipe of enablement has been plugged or clogged with grievous sin. Unplug the pipe (confession and cleansing), and the power will flow unimpeded once again (1 John 1:9). "Purge me with hyssop, and I shall be clean: wash me, and I shall be whiter than snow....*Then will I teach* transgressors thy ways; and *sinners shall be converted* unto thee" (Psalm 51:7,13). Paul's success in soulwinning was directly linked to the fact that no man could accuse him of unethical or immoral conduct (Acts 20:18).

d. Devotion. "Abide in Me, and I in you. As the branch cannot bear fruit of itself, except it abide in the vine; no more can ye, except ye abide in me" (John 15:4). Abiding in Christ is linked intrinsically to the infusion of supernatural power that is imperative to bearing fruit (being an effective witness). "To 'remain' [abide] in Jesus has a deeper significance than simply to continue to believe in Him, although it includes that; it connotes continuing to live in association or union with Him."[36] It means maintaining an intimate and loving relationship with Him at all costs. Horatius Bonar said, "A ministry of power must be the fruit of a holy, peaceful, loving intimacy with the Lord." Fredrick Robertson said, "Nothing can be love to GOD which does not shape itself into obedience."[37]

3. The Agency of the Holy Spirit.

Soulwinning is warfare. It is going into Satan's prison camp and rescuing souls held captive. Satan fears not man's wisdom, training, strategies, or strength in the effort, for they are futile against his powerhouse and stronghold. It is only by a power greater than his that he is forced to succumb, setting the captives to sin free. "Greater is he that is in you, than he that is in the world" (1 John 4:4). "Not by might, nor by power, but by my spirit" (Zechariah 4:6). The degree to which the soulwinner shares the Gospel rightly, is empty of self and sin, and is empowered with the Holy Spirit, will be the measure of the success experienced.

The Scottish evangelist Duncan Campbell said, "It is the signature of the Holy Ghost upon our work and witness that makes all the difference." Torrey declared, "The Holy Spirit is given to the individual believer for the definite purpose of witnessing for Christ."[38] Scarborough said, "Eloquence and charm of voice in song or speech may sweep men off their feet temporarily, but it takes the power of God to win them from their sins and regenerate them."[39] See Ephesians 5:18 and John 6:63. "Without the presence of the Spirit," states W. A. Criswell, "there is no conviction, no regeneration, no sanctification, no cleansing, no acceptable works....Life is in the quickening Spirit."[40] "A fisherman is a dependent person; he must look up for success every time he puts the net down."[41]

4. The Authority of God.

"All power is given unto me in heaven and in earth. Go ye therefore, and teach all nations, baptizing them in the name of the Father, and of the Son, and of the Holy Ghost" (Matthew 28:18–19). "In the name of" means "by the authority of." Zodhiates says, "Implying authority; e.g., to come or to do something in or by the name of someone, meaning using his name; as his messenger, envoy, representative; by his authority, with his sanction."[42] The messenger is divinely authorized to speak to man about his soul (Exodus 3:14).

Matthew Henry says, "It is He [Jesus] that qualifies men for this work, calls them to it, authorizes them in it, gives them a commission to fish for souls, and wisdom to win them."[43]

5. The Word of God.

"For no word from God shall be void of power" (Luke 1:37 ASV). Carry a pocket New Testament with you. "It is no heavier than a knife, but it is sharper than a two-edged sword."[44] The Bible is essential to soulwinning because it possesses God's message endowed with His power to break up the hardest soil, thwart the stubbornest of excuses, and save the worst of sinners. No other book in the world can do that. "Is not My word like as a fire? saith the Lord; and like a hammer that breaketh the rock in pieces?" (Jeremiah 23:29). Francis Dixon states, "The Lord always uses His Word to produce the miracle of conversion."[45] Spurgeon asserts, "We might preach 'til our tongue rotted, 'til we exhaust our lungs and die—but never a soul would be converted unless the Holy Spirit uses the Word to convert that soul. So it is blessed to eat into the very heart of the Bible until, at last, you come to talk in scriptural language and your spirit is flavored with the words of the Lord so that your blood is bibline and the very essence of the Bible flows from you."[46]

R. A. Torrey says, "A practical knowledge of the Bible involves four things: 1) A knowledge of how to so use the Bible as to show men and make men realize their need of a Savior. 2) A knowledge of how to use the Bible so as to show men Jesus as their Savior who meets their needs. 3) A knowledge of how to use the Bible so as to show men how to make Jesus their Savior. 4) A knowledge of the Bible so as to meet the difficulties that stand in the way of their accepting Christ."

6. A Marked New Testament.

Mark (map) the way to salvation in the New Testament in a "go to now" format. At the entry of the New Testament, write "Start with Romans 3:23." At that text, write on the top of the page, "Turn to Romans 6:23." At the top of its page, write "Turn to Romans 5:8." At the top of its page, write "Turn to Romans 10:9–13." And then, at its location, write "Turn to Revelation 3:20." (I began soulwinning using this approach.) Note, it is often good to have the prospect read aloud the texts as the presentation unfolds. Robert Murray McCheyne said, "It is not our comment on the Word that saves, but the Word itself."

7. Faith.

Confidence in God's ability to save the worst of sinners is essential. "But without faith it is impossible to please him" (Hebrews 11:6). Said Scarborough, "A restful faith in Christ's power and in the effectiveness of the Gospel will give a confident assurance of victory and will help vitalize every spiritual energy needful in winning men to Christ."[47]

Second, confidence in God's presence, power, and protection in soulwinning must be embraced. A. W. Pink states, "Faith is a grace which draws down from Heaven whatever blessing of God is most needful to the saint, and therefore does it stand him in as good stead in the night of adversity as in the day of prosperity. Faith imparts a steadfastness of purpose, a noble courage, and a tranquility of mind, which no human education or fleshly effort can supply. Faith makes the righteous as bold as a lion, refusing to recant though horrible tortures and a martyr's death be the only alternatives."[48]

8. Prayer.

E. M. Bounds said, "Talking to men for God is a great thing, but talking to God for men is greater still. He will never talk well and with real success to men for God who has not learned well how to talk to God for men."[49]

Says S. D. Gordon, "Man is a free agent, to use the old phrase, so far as God is concerned, utterly, wholly free. The purpose of our praying is not to force or coerce his will—never that. It is to *free* his will of the warping influences that now twist it awry. It is to get the dust out of his eyes so his sight shall be clear. And once he is free, able to see aright, to balance things without prejudice, the whole probability is in favor of his using his will to choose the only right."[50]

Fish and Conant state, "Prayer opens, and prayerlessness closes the channel between some lost soul and God."[51] Spurgeon says, "Prayer pulls the rope below, and the great bell rings above in the ears of God. Some scarcely stir the bell, for they pray so languidly [without energy or effort]. Others give but an occasional pluck at the rope. But he who wins with Heaven is the man who grasps the rope boldly and pulls continuously, with all his might."[52]

How to pray for the soulwinning visit

Scarborough states, "Prayer—constant, supplicating, importuning, soulful prayer—is God's key to His secret sources of power. Pray before, during, and after your efforts to win men. You cannot otherwise find your way successfully. Pray that your own heart will be right, your motive heavenly, your words wise, your heart burdened, that you may use the right Scripture. Pray that you may be led to the right person, that your method of approach will be right. Pray that God will go before you as He has promised (Isaiah 45:2). Pray that you may easily find the key to the soul of the unsaved. Pray for human tact and divine power. Pray that God will go behind you as He promises (Isaiah 58:8), that He will convert your mistakes into victories, override your errors, bring to full fruition the seed sown and the work sought to be accomplished."[53]

Billy Graham asserts, "Prayer is crucial in evangelism. Only God can change the heart of someone rebelling against Him. No matter how logical our arguments or how fervent our appeals are, our words will accomplish nothing unless God's Spirit prepares the way."[54]

How to pray for the lost sinner

Saith Oswald Sanders, "Plead the blood of the Lamb for the liberation of the soul for whom you pray."[55] Make a list of names of the lost for which to pray regularly (Romans 10:1). As some are saved, mark through the names, entering the dates of their conversion. Frequently add new names to the list. Such praying is profitable. In time, God will say, "I have heard thy prayer, I have seen thy tears" (Isaiah 38:5). Saith Spurgeon, "As Rachel cried, 'Give me children, or I die,' so may none of you be content to be barren. Cry and sigh until you have snatched some brand from the burning and have brought at least one sinner to Jesus Christ."[56] Sidlow Baxter declared, "Men may spurn our appeals, reject our message, oppose our arguments, despise our persons, but they are helpless against our prayers."

<u>Pray for the unsaved using Scripture</u>

*John 6:44*

Father, I ask in Jesus' name that You draw _____ to Yourself so that he might believe and be saved.

*2 Peter 3:9*

Father, I thank You that it's not Your will that ____ die lost to experience eternal separation from You in Hell, but that he might be saved. Quicken him unto salvation today.

*Matthew 13:1–9*

Father, orchestrate circumstances in ____ life today that somehow, by someone, the Word may be sown in his heart and be met with receptivity.

*Matthew 7:21*

O Lord, ____ professes to know You but is deceived by Satan. Open his eyes to the truth of his soul's condition so that he may acknowledge his lostness and be genuinely saved.

*Ephesians 2:1*

Lord Jesus, even as you quickened me when I was dead in trespasses and sin, please quicken ____ that he may know You as I do.

*1 Timothy 1:15*

Jesus, Your purpose in coming into the world was to save sinners. Please make this purpose known to ____, a sinner who needs Your forgiveness and grace.

*John 16:8*

Holy Spirit, it is Your divine work on earth to convict a lost man of his sin and need for salvation through Jesus Christ. Do this Thy office work in the heart of _____ today, I plead.

*Isaiah 64:6*

Heavenly Father, reveal to _____ that to trust in one's goodness for salvation is futile. Help him understand that his best righteousness is as a filthy rag in Your sight and that salvation is solely based on a relationship with You through Your Son, Jesus Christ.

*Romans 10:14*

Lord Jesus, _____ needs to hear a clear presentation of the Gospel and be given an opportunity to respond. Keep sending preachers, soulwinners, and Sunday school teachers to him until he hears, believes, and calls upon Your name in faith and repentance to be saved.

*Matthew 12:27–29*

Father, in Jesus' name, I ask that the strongman be bound in _____ life that he might believe and be set free.

*Isaiah 35:5*

Lord, under the preaching of the Word, please open the blind eyes and deaf ears of _____ to the truth about sin, judgment, and things to come that he might turn from sin unto Jesus Christ and be saved.

In learning he had only thirty minutes to live, a college president said, "Then take me out of bed and put me on my knees, and let me spend it on calling on God for the salvation of the world." This they did, and he died upon his knees. What a way to meet death!

9. Concern.

"Seeing the crowds, He felt compassion for them, because they were distressed and downcast, like sheep without a shepherd" (Matthew 9:36 NASB). A burden for the lost flows from Christ's concern and compassion for them to the believer who walks in close fellowship with Him. The disciples observed Jesus' agonies, tears, and passion for the lost and His efforts to win them, "and thus caught his spirit, and so they learned how to be fishers of men."[57] Spurgeon says, "Your battle-ax and weapons of war must come from the sacred connection with Christ. If you spend much time alone with Jesus, you will catch His spirit and be enflamed by the fire that engulfed His life. The power that stirred men's hearts and consciences in Him will be in your words, even if you cannot speak as eloquently as He did."[58] Pray that the weight of lost immortal souls (burden, concern, interest) that He possesses will be known experientially by you.

Lord, give me Thy love for souls,
For lost and wand'ring sheep,
That I may see the multitudes
And weep as Thou didst weep.

~Eugene M. Harrison

J. Hudson Taylor, while a college student, changed the dressing of a gangrenous foot of a non-Christian man who had not attended church for forty years. The man's hatred for the church was so intense he remained outside its doors at his wife's funeral. Taylor determined to witness to the man upon each visit and did, despite the man's cursing at him. A day came when the young student grew discouraged in the effort and said to himself as he was leaving the man's room, *It's no use.* But as he paused just before exiting, he saw the man looking at him as if to say, "Why are you going away today without speaking to me about Christ?" Taylor burst into tears, saying to the man, "Whether you wish me to or not, I must deliver my soul. Will you let me pray with you?" The man agreed, wept, and was converted. Later, Hudson Taylor said, "God broke my heart, that through me he might break this wicked man's heart." Pray for God to break your heart for damned souls so that through you, He may break their hearts for Him.

10. Soulwinning Companions.

Jesus, in seeing the value of a companion in soulwinning, sent both the twelve disciples (Mark 6:7) and the seventy (Luke 10:1) out two by two. Paul counted the practice important, teaming up in his soulwinning work with Barnabas (Acts 13:2) and later with Silas (Acts 15:40). Peter and John teamed up together (Acts 3:1). Barnabas and Mark went out two by two (Acts 15:39). Soulwinning companionship affords accountability, protection (from false accusation and harm), encouragement, courage, prayer support, backup under challenging encounters, distraction control in a witness, and exchanging ideas about the best approaches and methods. "It is very helpful," says Spurgeon, "to join in brotherly league with some earnest Christian who knows more than we do and will benefit us wise advice. God may bless us for the sake of others when He might not bless us for our own sake. The Spirit of God will bless two when He may not bless one."[59]

# 4
# The Soulwinners' Training

"And Jesus said unto them, Come ye after Me, and I will make [show, teach, instruct] you to become fishers of men" (Mark 1:17). Long ago, C. E. Matthews wrote, "Soulwinners are made. No Christian is a natural-born soulwinner. He must be developed in the art of winning others to Christ."[60] The skill or art of catching men is acquired or learned from abiding with the Master fisherman and following His example—the holy life that He lived, the concern that He showed, the people that He sought, the places that He went, the teaching that He taught, the power on which He depended (Acts 10:37–38), the way of His approach, the apologetics that He used, the pressing appeal that He presented, the sacrifices that He made, the persecution that He endured, and the constancy of His effort.

Saith Spurgeon, "Be Jesus-like. In all things, endeavor to think, speak, and act as Jesus did, and He will make you 'fishers of men.'"[61] The ability is sharpened or enhanced by the Holy Spirit's counsel (John 14:26), personal experience, and training. Said H. A. Ironside, "Soulwinning is not the slipshod business many would make it out to be—the mere hit-or-miss ministry that is so common today. On the contrary, it is a divine science requiring much earnest preparation of the heart in the presence of God and careful study of the need of the souls of men and of the truth of the Scriptures as given to meet that need."[62]

1. Soulwinning training involves knowledge of the plan of salvation. Whereas the soulwinner doesn't need a complete knowledge of theology, he must thoroughly know the plan of

salvation. Says Francis Dixon, "It is not enough to say, 'Come to Jesus!' They must be told who Jesus is, what He has done, what He is able to do, what it means to come to Him, and what the result of coming to Him will be."[63] The ready mind easily and quickly learns this knowledge.

2. Soulwinning training involves instruction in the basics. Though optional, an introductory study of the elementary mechanics of soulwinning is most profitable. This book is purposed to provide such training. "Give instruction to a wise man, and he will be still wiser; teach a righteous man, and he will increase in learning" (Proverbs 9:9 ESV). "The Lord God hath given me *the tongue of the learned*, that I should know how to speak a word in season to him that is weary" (Isaiah 50:4). The Christian can and should share the Gospel without "training." This is evident from the conversion of the blind man who, without any training or coaching, immediately testified, "One thing I know, that whereas I was blind, now I see" (John 9:25 KJ21).

Without training, the believer should be able to tell what God has done for him and how He did it. But with training, the ability to share the faith is sharpened and polished. In discussing the importance of tradesmen studying to know their trade, S. L. Brengle (Salvation Army) said, "How much more, then, should the soulwinner study in order that he may understand the diseases of the soul, the ramifications of evil, the deceitfulness of the human heart, and the application of the great remedy God has provided to meet all the needs of the soul! Or, to change the figure, how he must study to win his case at the bar of man's conscience when the man's own deceitful heart is the opposing counsel, assisted by that old adversary, the Devil, who for six thousand years has been deceiving the children of men and leading them down to Hell!"[64]

Charles Finney said, "Make it an object of constant study and daily reflection and prayer to learn how to deal with sinners to promote their conversion. It is the great business on earth of every Christian to save souls. People often complain that they do not know how to take hold of this matter. Why, the reason is plain enough: they have never studied it. They have never taken the proper pains to qualify themselves for the work. If people made it no more a matter of attention and thought to qualify themselves for their worldly business than they do to save souls, how do you think they would succeed? Now, if you are thus neglecting the main business of life, what are you living for?"[65]

3. Soulwinning training involves observation of the experienced. "Through observation, new visitors catch the spirit of soulwinning, as well as the knowledge of methods."[66]

Soulwinning is more easily caught than taught. "Iron sharpeneth iron" (Proverbs 27:17). Publilius Syrus said, "Observation, not old age, brings wisdom."

4. Soulwinning training involves participation in the task. The art of winning souls is mastered by its doing. "We learn to do by doing."[67] Experience is the best teacher. In going, we learn what works and doesn't; how to thwart fears, confront people, share effectively, and become comfortable sharing the faith. J. Oswald Sanders, after dealing with the traits and passion of the soulwinner in the book *The Divine Art of Soulwinning,* said, "The next step is to be found in II Samuel 3:18: 'Now then do it.' The art can be learned in no other way."

In agreement, E. Y. Mullins says, "Experience is a splendid teacher. One gradually acquires skill; and with skill, confidence; and with confidence, authority. Here it is especially true that practice makes perfect."[68] Moody's response to Torrey's inquiry about how to start soulwinning was short and simple, "Go at it!" With this, R. G. Lee agrees, saying, "Christians need to learn how to win the lost by going at it. We learn by doing. How do people learn to ride a bicycle? Not by milking cows but by giving themselves to bicycle riding. We learn to be fishers of men by fishing for men."[69]

5. Soulwinning training involves strategizing about the method. A *modus operandi* (methodology, technique) for confronting the unsaved must be developed and mentally fixed for ready recall at a moment's notice. Mastery of a method is developed through rehearsal (to family and friends) and recitation to the lost. Charles G. Finney said, "Make it an object of constant study and of daily reflection and prayer to learn how to deal with sinners to promote their conversion."

6. Soulwinning training involves a purification of the heart. Pivotal to usefulness and success in the task of winning souls is the holiness of the heart. Moody asserts, "God doesn't seek for golden vessels and does not ask for silver ones, but He must have clean ones." Therefore, the soulwinner should regularly learn to pray, "Search me, O God, and know my heart" (Psalm 139:23).

7. Soulwinning training involves memorization of pertinent texts. The memorization of the *key* why, how, where, and when verses of salvation improve the effectiveness of witnessing. The Word stored in the heart provides a ready witness in every circumstance (Psalm 119:11). "The mind stored with great Bible quotations becomes a powerful channel for the Holy Spirit to sweep through in bringing God's Word to the people."[70] Roland Q. Leavell says, "The more verses known, the more versatile the soulwinner will be."[71]

8. Soulwinning training involves navigation of the Holy Scriptures. The personal worker must be familiar with the Scriptures and how to maneuver from text to text with ease. What an opportunity Phillip would have squandered had he not been able to find the "place where it is written" in witnessing to the eunuch!

E. Y. Mullins stated of the soulwinner, "He should become so familiar with the pertinent passages of Scripture that he will be able to quote them from memory, and he should be at least sufficiently familiar with his Bible to be able to turn to any of these pertinent passages at will. The truth of God, as given to us in the Scriptures, is the sword of the Holy Spirit, and it is as this sword of the Spirit is unsheathed and wielded by the Christian that the Spirit can do his work in the heart."[72]

# 5

# The Soulwinners' Methods

On the great catch of fish in Luke 5:1–7, Spurgeon says, "The draught of fishes was miraculous, yet neither the fisherman nor his boat, [nor net] nor his fishing tackle were ignored; but all were used to take the fishes. So, in the saving of souls, God worketh by means."[73]

With soulwinning, there is no one way to do it. No one method fits all. Great latitude in witnessing techniques and plans is afforded. Leonard Ravenhill said, "Any method of evangelism will work if God is in it." William Booth said, "If I thought I could win one more soul to the Lord by walking on my head and playing the tambourine with my toes, I'd learn how!" Sherwood Wirt says, "God does not discriminate between methods of evangelism; he uses them all. Paul said he rejoiced in every way Christ was preached, and so should we."[74]

Note, Spurgeon asserts, "It is not our way of putting the Gospel, nor our method of illustrating it, which wins souls, but the Gospel itself does the work in the hands of the Holy Ghost, and to Him we must look for the thorough conversion of men."[75] A definite workable gospel presentation plan that is known well instills confidence and courage, as well as calm in and command of the witnessing encounter. Discover that plan and use it repeatedly with adaptation as necessary.

Whatever the method, the sinner must be told what he must do to be saved.

1. He must believe in who Jesus is and what He did at Calvary. "That if thou shalt confess with thy mouth the Lord Jesus, and shalt believe in thine heart that God hath raised Him from the dead, thou shalt be saved. For with the heart man believeth unto righteousness; and with the mouth confession is made unto salvation" (Romans 10:9–10). Belief must be expressed that Jesus is the Son of God who died on the Cross at Calvary and was raised from the dead to make forgiveness of sin and eternal life possible.

2. He must realize that he is lost. "For the Son of Man is come to seek and to save that which was lost" (Luke 19:10). Man must be saved because he is not saved already. He is lost by nature and is perishing (Ephesians 2:3). To be lost is to be estranged from the presence of God. To be lost is to be condemned to eternity in Hell. To be lost is to be shortchanged of the beautiful life God planned. To be lost is to be without purpose and peace. To be lost is to be without hope of Heaven. To be lost is to live life in rebellion against God. To

be lost is to be mastered and ravaged by sin. To be lost is to be under the rule of Satan.

He must understand that he can be saved. "Every one of them will come to me, and I will always accept them" (John 6:37 ICB). As none are good enough to be saved, none are too evil or sinful to be saved.[76] "We are made right with God by placing our faith in Jesus Christ. And this is true for everyone who believes, no matter who we are" (Romans 3:22 NLT).

3. He must want to be saved. "But as many as received him, to them gave he power to become the sons of God, even to them that believe on his name" (John 1:12). As salvation is freely offered, it must be willingly received. Others may and should encourage salvation, but ultimately, a person must personally decide for Christ. Comparing life without God to life with Him makes the choice apparent. Man must answer Pilate's question: 'What will you do with Jesus?'

4. He must make a personal response to the offer of salvation. "The necessary response may be described as a complete change of allegiance on man's part from sin to God and a trusting committal of self to God."[77] That is, it involves faith (Ephesians 2:8–9) and repentance (Acts 17:30).

"Saving faith," states C. E. Autrey, "is a trustful surrender of one's entire being, and destiny into the hands of God."[78] Repentance is intertwined with saving faith and is inseparable from it. When people believe in Christ for salvation, they simultaneously turn from (repenting of) their unbelief and sin.[79] John Murray says, "Saving faith is permeated with repentance, and repentance is permeated with saving faith."[80] They are two sides of the same coin.[81] Spurgeon asserts, "True belief and true repentance are twins. It would be idle to attempt to say which is born first."[82]

**Ways to bring souls to Christ**

1. The Roman Road Plan.

It was the use of this method that I cut my teeth on as a teenager in soulwinning.

Underline the verses to be used and mark them sequentially in a New Testament for easy navigation. First, write on the flyleaf of the

New Testament, the starting text of Romans 3:10–12. At Romans 3:10–12, at the top margin of the page, write "turn to Romans 3:23." At Romans 3:23, at the top margin of the page, write "turn to Romans 6:23a." At Romans 6:23, at the top margin of the page, write "turn to Romans 5:8." At Romans 5:8, at the top margin of the page, write "turn to Romans 6:23b." At Romans 6:23, at the top margin of the page, write "turn to Romans 10:8–13."

*Tell* the prospect that you would like to use several texts in the book of Romans to explain how a person may become right with God and experience an abundant and meaningful life now and in Heaven with God at death.

*Step One.* Tell the prospect that none are righteous in God's sight. "As it is written, there is none righteous, no, not one" (Romans 3:10). Explain that the verse states that no person is righteous (without sin). Say, "If no person is righteous, that means that I'm not, your wife is not, your neighbor is not, and you are not. Isn't that so?"

*Step Two.* Tell the prospect that all have sinned. "All have sinned, and come short of the glory of God" (Romans 3:23). This verse reinforces the previous verse, driving home the point of personal sin. Point out that sin is the failure to measure up to the holy standards of God, the Ten Commandments. Ask the prospect if he has ever broken a commandment. He will reply that he has violated not just one but many. Ask, "In light of that, what does that make you?" The reply will be a sinner.

A man must first realize that he is a sinner before he will see the need to be saved. Note, most Americans (67 percent) agree with Romans 3:23 but disagree on how to handle it.[83] We must bring them to realize that the only solution to the sin problem is a personal relationship with Jesus Christ—not reform, righteousness, good deeds, or religion (1 John 1:7, 9; Romans 5:8).

*Step Three.* Tell the prospect the consequence of sin. "The wages of sin is death" (Romans 6:23a). Explain that the word "wages" means payment for something deserved for something done. Tell the prospect that we all deserve, because of sinful rebellion against God, an eternity of separation from God in a place called Hell. Say, "BUT I have some great news for you!"

*Step Four*. Tell the prospect the remedy for sin. "But God commendeth his love toward us, in that, while we were yet sinners, Christ died for us" (Romans 5:8). This is the heart of the presentation. Share it especially with excitement and joy. Tell your prospect that Jesus died the death at Calvary and was raised from the dead to make possible man's forgiveness, rightness with God, and eternal life. Share how He paid the sin debt we owed, so we don't have to pay it. Ask the person why he thinks that God did this for man. Say, "The answer is clear. It was out of His great love for man." You may want to share John 3:16 at this point. "For God so loved the world, that he gave his only begotten Son, that whosoever believeth in him should not perish, but have everlasting life."

*Step Five*. Tell the prospect that salvation is to be received as a free gift. "But the gift of God is eternal life through Jesus Christ our Lord" (Romans 6:23b). Pardon of sin and eternal life (salvation) is a gift. As a gift, it cannot be purchased by man. There is nothing man can do to merit it. Goodness, merit, works, baptism, or church membership cannot attain it. It is strictly a gift.

*Step Six*. Tell the prospect how the gift of salvation is received. "That if thou shalt confess with thy mouth the Lord Jesus, and shalt believe in thine heart that God hath raised him from the dead, thou shalt be saved. For with the heart man believeth unto righteousness; and with the mouth confession is made unto salvation....For whosoever shall call upon the name of the Lord shall be saved" (Romans 10:9, 10, 13). Share that the gift of forgiveness of sin and eternal life is to be received by faith (believing trust, reliance in Christ), repentance (willingness to turn from sin to Christ), and request (the asking of Christ for it).

*Step Seven*. Briefly review all that was said, asking if it is understood. *Now* ask this question, "Is there any good reason why you cannot receive Christ's gift of forgiveness and eternal life, receiving Him into your life as Lord and Savior?" After a momentary pause, say, "I know you agree that there are no good reasons for delaying such an important decision." Upon the prospect's willingness to be saved, kneel with him (if possible and practicable) and lead him in the sinner's prayer. (If the person hesitates to make the decision, share 2 Corinthians 6:2b: "Behold, now is the accepted time; behold, now is the day of salvation," warning of the danger of delay.)

*Tell* the new convert how he may be assured of salvation. Question: "What did you ask Jesus Christ to do for you?" Answer: "I asked Him to come into my life and forgive me." Question: "Do you believe He did?" Answer: "Not sure." Say, "Read Romans 10:13 and share what Jesus promises." Answer: "Jesus promises to save all those who call upon His name." Question: "Did you call upon His name in that way?" Answer: "Yes, I did." Question: "Then, according to the promise, what happened?" Answer: "Jesus saved me." Say, "Jesus dogmatically states that if you call upon Him from a heart of godly sorrow and belief to be saved, that will undoubtedly happen (Romans 10:13; John 1:12)."

You can share Revelation 3:20 to drive the point further home. "Behold, I stand at the door, and knock: if any man hear my voice, and open the door, I will come in to him, and will sup [fellowship] with him, and he with me." Jesus knocks at our heart's door for entrance. When we open it and invite Him to enter, He promises to come in immediately to stay forever. Question: "Did you hear Christ's knock at your heart's door and, in response, open it to allow Him entry?" Answer: "Yes, I did." Question: "Then what did He promise to do?" Answer: "To come into my life and save me."

### 2. Personal Testimony Plan.

John wrote, "We proclaim to you what we have seen and heard" (1 John. 1:3 NIV). Perhaps the most powerful tool in witnessing is your salvation story, how Jesus transformed your life. Roland Q. Leavell said, "It is experience, not logic, which grips the heart of a seeking sinner. To tell one's spiritual experience is more convincing than a thousand theories."[84] Adrian Rogers said, "A Christian with a testimony is never at the mercy of an unbeliever with an argument, because the Christian has the witness in himself."[85]

### A. How to Prepare a Testimony

Prayerfully seek the Holy Spirit's guidance about what to include in it. Organize it. Refine it for brevity (three to four minutes) and clarity (omit churchy words). Write it out. Rehearse it with friends to the point that it becomes natural to tell. Restrict it to one main thought that flows throughout your presentation. Share the highlights of your journey with Christ from start to now, not specifics. Include pertinent Bible verses. Stick with your talking points; don't stray. Don't demean others. Don't glorify sin. Don't make the Christian life a bed of roses without trials or troubles.

B. How to Share a Testimony

Spurgeon advised, "Oh! when we tell the story of our own conversion, I would have it done with great sorrow, remembering what we used to be, and with great joy and gratitude, remembering how little we deserve these things."[86]

The Apostle Paul's testimony unto Agrippa is a worthy testimonial pattern (Acts 26:3–29).

Introduction: Use an attention-grabbing statement. Example: "My life was empty and meaningless until I made life's greatest discovery."

(1) My life before meeting Christ (Acts 26:3–11). Share what was missing in your life or its emptiness, meaninglessness, or deception before salvation. What futile efforts were taken to meet these needs? Speak of past sins or bad habits briefly, if warranted, but without specificity. Around what things did your life revolve?

(2) How I realized my need for Christ (Acts 26:12–14). What influenced you to become a Christian (search for meaning, purpose, or peace in life, etc.)? Share the circumstances that surrounded your decision to follow Christ. Was it a sermon, a chapel talk at camp, a relationship, an addiction, an accident, an illness, or an encounter with a soulwinner?

(3) What I did to become a Christian (Acts 26:15–18). Share how you became a Christian. "At that point, my heart was crushed with the weight of my sins and the need of Jesus. I walked down the aisle to the altar, where I knelt and asked Jesus to forgive and save me." Make clear the exact how of your salvation.

(4) My life since I became a Christian (Acts 26:19–23). Share how Jesus has supplied your needs and blessed you beyond measure. Share what you count to be the most beautiful part of your

relationship with Jesus. Share the changes Jesus made to your life (2 Corinthians 5:17).

(5) Give an appeal to receive Christ. Share an earnest request to the person to become a Christian. Example: "Would you be willing to do as I did and receive Christ into your life as Lord and Savior? (Acts 26:27–29). You can now pray with me what I did long ago, the sinner's prayer."

C. Where to Share a Testimony

Look for opportunities to share it—over coffee with an unsaved friend, classmate, or fellow worker; during church visitation; or at a church service. Share it while waiting in a grocery store line, getting a haircut, at a social outing with a friend, or while traveling on public transportation.

3. The Gospel Tract Ladder Plan.

It begins with the elementary stage of sharing the Gospel (bottom rung) and progresses to the most challenging rung.[87]

Share a Tract
Share the synopsis of the tract with the purpose of winning to Christ.

Lend a Tract
Loan a tract/book; upon return ask for impressions.

Hand a Tract
Give tracts to people met in passing— restaurant servers, cashiers, etc.

Pin and Tract
Wear a bold badge that prompts inquiry; answer, "It reminds me to give you this tract."

Mail a Tract
Insert in correspondence/payments/cards

Leave a Tract
Place in restrooms, laundromats, bus/airline terminals, restaurants, motel rooms.

Mitsuo Fuchida, the Japanese commander who shouted the war cry "Tora, Tora, Tora" at Pearl Harbor, became a Christian by reading the New Testament. It was an uncomplicated Gospel tract, however, that prompted him to purchase it. What if Jacob DeShazer had not handed him the tract?[88]

Hudson Taylor picked up a gospel tract in his father's library, hoping to find an exciting story. The phrase "the finished work of Christ" grasped his attention, causing him to ask himself, *What is finished?* Understanding that Christ's death completely paid the debt of man's sin and the work necessary for salvation was finished, all that remained for him to do was accept it. And that he did immediately upon his knees. Later it was discovered that his mother was driven to pray for his salvation at that same hour in another town.[89]

"The Bruised Reed" (gospel tract), written by Richard Sibbs, was the means of conversion to a little boy named Richard Baxter, who wrote "Call to the Unconverted," which brought Philip Doddridge and others to Christ.

Saith Spurgeon, "When preaching and private talk are unavailable, you need to have a tract ready. But *a touching gospel tract may be the seed of eternal life.* Therefore, do not go out without your tracts."[90] Not all gospel tracts are created equal. Some are theologically flawed or weak in the gospel presentation, deceitful in appearance, or unappealing in design (fish must be drawn to the bait before they will bite). Spurgeon advises, "Some tracts would not convert a beetle; there is not enough in them to interest a fly. Get good striking tracts or none at all."[91]

### 4. Gospel Booklet Plan.

Gospel booklets present the steps to salvation that may be read to the prospect or highlighted for him. "The Four Spiritual Laws" (Campus Crusade), "Steps to Peace with God" (Billy Graham), "Would You Like to Know God as Your Friend" (Carl Broggi), and "False Hopes of Heaven" (the author's) are time-tested effective witnessing booklets.

## 5. Evangelistic Letters.

An evangelistic letter will bear the gospel message if distance or incarceration inhibits a visit. Roland Q. Leavell stated, "A postage stamp is a mighty ally in soulwinning. In a letter, one can write smoothly and succinctly the essential things of salvation which the unsaved man should believe and accept."[92]

Spurgeon said, "Paper and ink are never better used than in soulwinning."[93] Share your testimony or a gospel presentation, keeping it simple, straightforward, non-condemning, and brief. Enclose a gospel tract.

### Lifestyle Evangelism vs. Confrontational Evangelism Methods

Lifestyle Evangelism is the belief that living the Christian life before men (observation by the lost) "satisfies the demands of the Great Commission."[94] But such a view is wrong. The Great Commission calls for verbal communication of the Gospel. It states, "Go ye into all the world, and *preach the gospel* to every creature" (Mark 16:15). The Greek word for "preach" is *euangelizo*—"to preach/proclaim the good news," an oral communication of the Gospel. The believer's walk without his talk is theologically flawed evangelism.

Paul says, "For whosoever shall call upon the name of the Lord shall be saved. How then shall they call on him in whom they have not believed? And how shall they believe in him of whom they have not heard? and how shall they hear without a preacher?" (Romans 10:13–14). Nowhere is it stated in Scripture that a person was saved by observing Jesus' perfect life, only by hearing His Word.

Donald Whitney tells the story of a man who was converted at a crusade. When he shared the news with his boss, the employer said, "That's great! I am a Christian and have been praying for you for years!"

Disappointedly, the new believer replied, "Why didn't you ever tell me? You were the very reason I have not been interested in the Gospel all these years."

The boss wondered, "How can that be? I have done my very best to live the Christian life around you."

Replying, the man said, "That's the point. You lived such a model life without telling me that it was Christ who made the difference. I convinced myself that if you could live such a good and happy life without Christ, then I could too."[95] Living an exemplary life is imperative, but couple it with an oral presentation of the gospel.

# 6

# The Soulwinners' Promise

Jesus said, "I am with you always, even unto the end of the world" (Matthew 28:20).

*The promise of Christ's presence.* He is Emmanuel, "God with us" (Matthew 1:23). "The power and inspiration of missionary work is His presence in our midst."[96] Matthew Henry said, "To carry them [the disciples then, all believers now] on through the difficulties they were likely to meet, Jesus says, 'I am with you, to bear you up, to plead your cause; with you in all your services, in all your sufferings, to bring you through them with comfort and honor. When you go through the fire or water, I will be with you. In the pulpit, in the prison, lo, I am with you. Lo, I am with you to make your ministry effectual for the discipling of the nations, for the pulling down of the strongholds of Satan, and the setting up of stronger for the Lord Jesus."[97]

John Trapp says, "When Christ saith, 'I am with you alway,' you may add what you will: to protect you, to direct you, to comfort you, to carry on the work of grace in you, and in the end to crown you with immortality and glory. All this and more are included in this precious promise."[98]  Francis Dixon says, "The most glorious assurance we have as we engage in this work is the confidence that the Lord is always there before us in His knowledge of and concern for the soul we are seeking to win."

*The promise of Christ's power.* "But ye shall receive power, after that the Holy Ghost is come upon you: and ye shall be witnesses unto me both in Jerusalem, and in all Judaea, and in Samaria, and unto the uttermost part of the earth" (Acts 1:8). "Note, Christ's witnesses shall receive power for that work to which He calls them; those whom He employs in His service He will qualify for it and will bear them out in it."[99] With the power of the Holy Spirit to break the hardest and stubbornest heart, subdue the most rebellious will, enlighten the darkest mind to the Gospel truth, and thwart the fiercest of opposition and difficulties, the most ordinary believer can do the extraordinary as a fisher of men.

*The promise of Christ's participation.* "And they went out and preached everywhere, *the Lord working with them*" (Mark 16:20 NKJV). Despite others' receptivity or ridicule, we may confidently do the job of winning souls, knowing the Lord is working with us. And if He is working with us in the harvest field, what is there to dread, fear, or flee? At the end of the race, the soulwinner may say with Paul, who, while housed in a cold and dark Roman dungeon, "The Lord stood with me, and strengthened me; that by me the preaching might be fully known, and that all the Gentiles might hear" (2 Timothy 4:17). There's a double reason why Christ stands mightily with and for us. First, because we are His children (1 John 3:1). Second, because of the message we bear to the world (Acts 20:21; Matthew 28:18–19). See Luke 10:19 and Job 5:19.

> He knows how I am longing
> Some weary soul to win,
> And so He bids me go and speak the loving word for Him;
> He bids me tell His wondrous love
> And why He came to die,
> And so we work together, My Lord and I.
>
> ~L. Shorey (1890)

*The promise of productiveness* (success). "He that goeth forth and weepeth, bearing precious seed, shall doubtless come again with rejoicing, bringing his sheaves with him" (Psalm 126:6). "The principle of sowing and reaping, which is applicable to the restoration of the exiles, also serves as an encouragement to all believers to be faithful in personal witnessing."[100] Saith Spurgeon, "*Doubtlessly,* you will gather sheaves from your sowing. Because the Lord has written *doubtless*, take heed that you do not doubt. No reason for doubt can remain after the Lord has spoken."[101] Again Spurgeon says, "With sheaves—as an old expositor says, he comes with the wains behind him, with the wagons at his heels. They are his sheaves, for though all souls belong to Christ, they yet belong to the worker. God puts it so, 'bringing his sheaves with him.' Christ assures you of this. Think, too, of those who have already proved it. See the triumphs of missions. Therefore, be up and doing."[102] *Doubtless*—"There is no contingency, no mere 'perhaps'; his 'labor is not in vain in the Lord.' Faithful toil shall not fail of a reward."[103] The sacred seed sown sometimes springs up immediately and other times after a long delay of slumber in the soul. "Those men always come back to God with their sheaves who went from God with their seed."[104] See Ecclesiastes 11:1, Isaiah 55:11, and 2 Corinthians 9:6.

# 7
# The Soulwinners' Appeal

Soulwinning often breaks down at one of its most pivotal and crucial points, its climax. It stops short of inviting the prospect to become a Christian. When all the tilling, sowing, and cultivating steps are done, it's time to reap. John declared, "And the Spirit and the bride say, 'Come.' And let him that heareth say, 'Come.' And let him that is athirst come; and whosoever will, let him take the Water of Life freely" (Revelation 22:17 KJ21).

The Christian must join the Spirit in saying to the sinner, "Come." In the Great Commission, Jesus underscores this "must" in saying, "Make disciples" (Matthew 28:19 ASV). We "make disciples" by proclaiming the truth about Jesus to sinners and inviting them to receive Him as Lord and Savior. It's not enough to tell a man the gospel story. A way must be opened in the pulpit and personal witnessing for man to respond to the offer of forgiveness of sin and reconciliation with God.

Witnessing is sharing Christ by walking, talking, and writing. Soulwinning encompasses the same but includes an invitation, a kite tail at its end, to be saved. Most believers are witnesses; few are soulwinners.

"In our work of evangelism," states J. I. Packer, "Christians are sent to convert. Evangelizing includes the endeavor to elicit a response to the truth taught. It is communication with a view to conversion. It is a matter not merely of informing but also of inviting. It is an attempt to *gain* or *win* or *catch* our fellow men for Christ (1 Corinthians 9:19–23; 1 Peter 3:1; Luke 5:10). Our Lord depicts it as fishermen's work (Matthew 4:19; 13:47)."[105] Spurgeon asserts, "Our great aim is conversion—the conversion of transgressors. Be content with nothing short of the conversion of men."[106]

Peter's net fishing pictures the soulwinner's invitation (Luke 5:1–7). The net had to be cast into the water in quest of fish and retrieved to be profitable. No matter how expertly crafted, designed, or used, the net would have availed naught without Peter's effort or attempt to pull it back into the boat. (Sometimes help is needed in dealing with all that respond to the invitation—Luke 5:7).

Application: the soulwinner's net (the Gospel) is always in the boat with him. However, it is only when it is *thrust into the water* of lost humanity (proclaimed, presented, declared) and *retrieved* (invitation, "What will you do with Jesus?") that its supreme and fullest purpose is realized—the catching of fish.

"It is not enough," asserts William Evans, "to answer the inquirer's questions, to dissolve his doubts, or to enlighten his ignorance. All this the worker may do and still leave the man unsaved. To leave the inquirer with the question of accepting Jesus Christ as his personal Savior settled—this is the aim and end of all personal dealing."[107]

Charles L. Goodell said, "It is a great hour when a surgeon holds a scalpel at the end of which is life or death for the patient. It is a greater hour when a lawyer faces a jury with a conviction that if he makes a mistake, an innocent man will hang and a family be disgraced forever. But the greatest hour any human being ever faces is when he stands before a man hastening to his condemnation and is commissioned to offer him a pardon that will last for eternity." We must do our very best in such an hour.

### At the climax of the Gospel presentation

1. Encapsulate what it is to trust Christ as Lord and Savior.

To receive Jesus Christ as Lord and Savior is to wholeheartedly trust Him for the forgiveness of sins, reconciliation with God, and eternal life based upon His atoning death and resurrection, and to commit the entire life to His governance.

2. Transition to the appeal (invitation) by asking a question. Presented here are three suggestions.

- "Is there any good reason you couldn't receive Christ now as your Lord and Savior?" If he responds, "No," then ask him to take your hand as a sign of faith and pray to receive Christ.

- "In light of what I have shared, would you be willing to receive Christ as Lord and Savior? If so, I will lead you in the 'sinner's prayer.' There is nothing magical about the prayer, but if it is meant, Christ surely will answer with saving power."

- "Jesus is knocking at your heart's door, seeking entrance to forgive and save you. Will you this moment open the door, inviting Him to enter through prayer?"

3. Lead them to pray the sinner's prayer.

"Jesus, I believe You died at Calvary and were raised from the dead to make my forgiveness, rightness with God, and everlasting life possible. In turning from my sins, I now invite You into my heart to be my Lord and Savior."

E. Y. Mullins provides excellent advice when calling for a decision. "The first rule is to be sure to make the proposition clear. To ask the inquirer to do two or three things at the same time—things that are not identical but which resemble each other—tends to leave the mind of the inquirer confused. Of course, it may be proper occasionally to put two propositions together, but as a rule, it is wiser to make one appeal and make it very clear so that it cannot be misunderstood, than it is to include two or three."[108] Accept whatever decision is made at face value. Whether it is authentic or disingenuous will become manifest in due time. "Do not make a definite proposal and, when it is accepted, act as if you doubted the genuineness of the acceptance."[109]

# 8

# The Soulwinners' Persuasion

Clark Pinnock stated, "The notion that nobody is ever converted to Christ by argument [not quarrel, but reasoning defense] is a foolish platitude."[110] The subject of persuasion is absent in many books on soulwinning (evangelism) but is pivotal to its success. Solomon said, "Patient persuasion can break down the strongest resistance and can even convince rulers" (Proverbs 25:15 GNT).

The soulwinners' task is "Persuading them concerning Jesus" (Acts 28:23). Paul said, "Knowing therefore the terror of the Lord, we persuade men" (2 Corinthians 5:11). And this Paul did, "arguing persuasively" (Acts 19:8–10 NIV). D. E. Garland states, "Persuading others is part of what God has called Paul [and every believer] to do as one charged with a message of reconciliation."[111] Saith Spurgeon, "You are not only witnesses; you are also pleaders of the Lord Jesus Christ."[112]

Persuasion is "to prevail upon or win over, to bring about a change of mind by the influence of reason or moral considerations."[113] Persuasion is not pressure or manipulation, but a sound rationale put to the unbeliever as a reason to believe in Christ and follow Him. It is a convincing truth or argument (apologetics) that Jesus is the Son of God who died at Calvary to make possible man's forgiveness from the penalty of sin and man's needed acceptance of Him as Lord and Savior through repentance and faith.

The soulwinners' motivation in persuading man to be saved is the same as Paul's—the future judgment of God upon sin and unbelief and its resultant consequences, torment in an eternal Hell. Years ago, C. E. Matthews wrote, "The wrath of God upon the sin of unbelief stirs the Christian to persuade the lost to come to Christ for salvation."[114]

*The skeptical.*

How might the skeptical lost be convinced or persuaded that Christ is all He claims and that they have need of faith in Him? "According to God's standards, not with the trappings of a gilded rhetoric or with seductive trickery."[115] A man convinced against his will is unconvinced still. Man is to be persuaded by showing there is nothing unreasonable in belief in Christ and His teachings, by showing abundant evidence for its validity[116] biblically, historically, and in personal experience. The purpose of persuasion is to convince the skeptic that embracing the Christian faith is reasonable and proper (Acts 17:17–18). "Faith in Christianity," wrote Paul Little, "is based on evidence. It is a reasonable faith. Faith in the Christian sense goes beyond reason but not against it."[117]

*The hesitant.*

How might the "believing" lost man be convinced to respond immediately to Christ's invitation to salvation? That is, how can we, as Spurgeon said, "persuade those persons who believe the truth notionally, and yet do not receive it in their hearts"?[118] By showing reasons for their immediate need and the danger of delay.

An effective persuasion to salvation is fear of the wrath of God when presented lovingly and compassionately. "Knowing therefore the terror of the Lord, we persuade men" (2 Corinthians 5:11). "Paul had no delight in terrifying men; but he felt that if he could once bring men to feel a dread of the punishment of sin, they would be better disposed to hearken to the gentle voice of the Gospel. Thus, we seek to 'persuade men.' We feel that to make men shun destruction, we must make them aware of its fearfulness."[119] "It is a fearful thing to fall into the hands of the living God" (Hebrews 10:31).

Curtis Hutson reminds us that "men are not only loved into Heaven; they are also warned into it. 'Noah...moved with fear, prepared an ark.' [Hebrews 11:7]"[120] Eighty law, medical, or engineering students were asked, "How many of you gave your hearts to Christ simply through your great love for God?" None stated that they did. Then they were asked, "How many of you gave your hearts to Christ because you knew there was an awful Hell from which to flee and that without a Sin-bearer, you would be eternally lost?" Each of the students indicated that was how Christ won them.[121]

It was such persuasion that Jonathan Edwards used in the sermon "Sinners in the Hands of an Angry God" that swept many into the kingdom. It was such persuasion that Spurgeon utilized in the sermon "Loving Persuasion," where he said, "I must persuade you with all my heart to come to Jesus, for if you perish in the light, you will perish with a vengeance. If you go down to destruction from the borders of salvation, it will be sevenfold destruction. If you die with Jesus weeping over you, as he did over Jerusalem, you will die horribly!"[122] Similarly, J. Harold Smith used it in the sermon "God's Three Deadlines."

In personal encounters with the lost, the soulwinner will be wise to use what these ministers employed in sermons effectively and compassionately. Spurgeon said, "God has ordained both the terrors of the law and the tenderness of the Gospel, that by means of both, men may be saved. Gospel husbandry employs many implements, and there are some lands which will never yield a harvest without much more exercising with the plow than others may require."[123]

Persuasion power flows from the Holy Spirit. Trust Him to supply it. And it flows from a heart that knows the truth (1 Peter 3:15) and the terror of the Lord (2 Corinthians 5:11). John Ruskin said, "He who has truth at his heart need never fear the want of persuasion on his tongue."[124] The bottom line is that to be effective, personal persuasiveness must be enveloped in the gospel message, energized by the Holy Spirit, and void of trickery and pressure.

Presentation to the lost of the most compelling reasons for salvation shared articulately and passionately will often avail, but not always. Recall that Agrippa responded to Paul's powerful witness by saying, "Thou almost persuadest me to be a Christian" (Acts 26:28 KJ21). See Acts 28:23–24. If the Holy Spirit does not persuade a man to believe on account of the gospel's truthfulness, the biblical record, present need, and future judgment, doubtless anything else will genuinely convince him.

With this assertion, Spurgeon agrees, saying, "If the voice of God from the top of Sinai and His voice by Moses in the book of the Law, if His voice by the divers [various] prophets in the Old Testament, and especially His own word by His own Son, who hath brought immortality to light by the Gospel, cannot convince men, then there is nothing in the world that can of itself accomplish the work."[125] See John 6:44.

# 9

# The Soulwinners' Approach

How might the believer initiate a gospel conversation with the lost? Saith Scarborough, "The matter of approach, tactfulness in seeking an entrance for the gospel message, is very important. Sometimes it is best to adopt indirect methods of approach, come up on the 'blind side'; sometimes, the direct method is best. Here, tact, common sense, is of great value."[126] An accessible approach to every human heart exists; look prayerfully and patiently for it.[127]

1. The use of questions.

Phillip's question to the eunuch, "Do you understand what you are reading?" (Acts 8:30 ESV), led to a spiritual conversation that resulted in the man's salvation. Easy-to-remember questions will serve as an excellent launchpad to sharing the faith.

*Suggested questions to use to initiate a gospel conversation*

"Do you give much thought to God and spiritual matters?"

"Are you interested in spiritual things?"

"Have you come to a place in your spiritual life where you can say you know for certain that if you were to die today, you would go to Heaven?"

"What church do you attend in the area?"

"May I tell you about something that has meant more to me than anything else in life?"[128]

"Have you heard of the Four Spiritual Laws?"

"Do you know for sure that you will go to Heaven one day?"[129]

"May I ask you an unanswerable question? It's the question of Hebrews 2:3. 'How shall we escape if we neglect so great salvation; which at first began to be spoken by the Lord, and was confirmed unto us by them that heard him.'"

"If you were to die today and stand before God and He were to ask you, 'Why should I let you into My Heaven,' what would you say?"

"Has anybody ever taken the Bible and showed you how a person might become a Christian and gain Heaven at death?"

"Would you like to know for certain that you would go to Heaven at death?"

"Is there anything I can pray for you about when I say the blessing for the meal?" (To waiters, waitresses)

"Are you a Christian?"

"If you died within 24 hours, where would you be in eternity? Heaven or Hell?" (known as "The Frank Jenner question," since he asked it to many people)

2. The Pray and Say approach.

"We are out on the streets today sharing the love of God and praying for people. What might I pray with you about?"

3. The use of gospel tracts.

Handing a tract to the prospect, ask, "May I take a few moments to share what it says?"

4. The use of something the prospect says.

Many doors open to a witness by riding piggyback on something the sinner says. At a doctor's office, the nurse noted that she and I shared the same birthday. Immediately, I replied, "I have two birthdays; how about you?

She was at first puzzled by the reply and then said, "You mean born-again?"

"Yes," I said and made a witness for Christ.

5. The use of questionnaires or surveys.

"I am doing a three-question questionnaire for my church today about people's beliefs. Do you have a moment to participate?"

6. The use of a current or past event.

Concerning the tragic death of the Columbia astronauts, President Bush (#43) said that though they did not return to earth, "We pray that they safely arrived at Home." Upon sharing that with the prospect, say, "What do you think is necessary for a person to arrive at Home (Heaven) safely?"

7. The use of a button or badge.

Wear a bright, colorful button, and, when asked its meaning, say, "It reminds me to tell you how much Jesus loves you." Wear a lapel pin etched with the word "If" and when asked its meaning say, "If you were to die tonight, would you go to Heaven?"

8. Listening.

"I have found," states John Bisagno, "that the easiest way to get into a discussion about the things of God is to listen. In almost any conversation, people will say something that you can pick up on and turn into spiritual talk. They will ask a leading question. They may bring up a topic with a spiritual implication. But if you will listen with your heart, you will find the Holy Spirit opening doors big enough to drive trucks through."[130]

# 10

# The Soulwinners' Thinking

Think like a soulwinner. "For as he thinketh in his heart, so is he" (Proverbs 23:7). Thinking (believing) like a soulwinner keeps the mind alert to the many opportunities to witness.

A soulwinner thinks that no one is beyond the reach of salvation. A soulwinner thinks not of a man's appearance, garments, or gold, but of the state of his soul. A soulwinner thinks sinners secretly yearn for something more to life than what they know. A soulwinner

47

thinks the lost depends on him to point him to Jesus. A soulwinner thinks his witness may be a person's last chance to be saved.

A soulwinner thinks he has a great ally (the Holy Spirit) working in sinners for their salvation. A soulwinner thinks, despite his frailties, fear, and impotence, that the Holy Spirit will empower him in Jesus' name to march into the enemy's camp and free the captives. A soulwinner thinks the Holy Spirit ordains divine encounters or appointments, like that of Phillip and the eunuch. A soulwinner thinks the Holy Spirit can use the feeblest and frailest to convert the wickedest. A soulwinner thinks he possesses the power of the Holy Spirit, making soul-winning miracles possible to everyone, everywhere.

A soulwinner thinks that Hell is a place of terror and torment for the soul who dies without Christ. A soulwinner thinks a soul is worth one's best effort and sacrifice to win. A soulwinner thinks every person met is a soul for which Christ died. A soulwinner thinks the Gospel should be woven into as many conversations with the unsaved as possible.

A soulwinner thinks that prayer avails mightily in the warfare for souls. A soulwinner thinks that God will protect and sustain him in labor for souls. A soulwinner thinks that the Gospel is so powerful that if a man gives place to its presentation, he will be saved.

A soulwinner thinks that the best thing to be done for Jesus is to win souls. A soulwinner thinks a transformed life (not honor, recognition, or accolade) is sufficient payment for a witness presented.

Thinking like a soulwinner, John Wesley said, "I desire to have both Heaven and Hell in my eye." Thinking like a soulwinner, Mark Cahill said, "If they are breathing…they need Jesus." Thinking like a soulwinner, David Brainerd said, "I cared not how or where I lived or what hardships I went through so that I could gain souls for Christ. While I was asleep, I dreamed of these things, and when I awaked, the first thing I thought of was this great work." Thinking like a soulwinner, Nicolaus Zinzendorf said, "I have but one passion—it is He; it is He alone. The world is the field, and the field is the world, and henceforth that country shall be my home where I can be most used in winning souls for Christ." Thinking like a soulwinner, Scarborough said, "I want to win all the lost ones to Jesus that I can while I have life and strength, and then as death opens the gates of Heaven, lead some soul to Christ." Thinking like a soulwinner, Sam Jones said, "If I had a thousand tongues, they should all talk for Christ; a thousand hands, they should all work for Christ; a thousand feet, I'd put them in the way to Heaven."[131]

Cultivate and discipline your mind to think like a soulwinner. "Renew the thinking in your mind by the Spirit" (Ephesians 4:23 CEB).

# 11

# The Soulwinners' Fear

Soulwinning is a frightening endeavor that paralyzes duty. But this fear is conquerable. How?

1. The fear of being unsuccessful in soulwinning is thwarted by knowing that God, not us, is responsible for the results. Our part is to share the Gospel in the power of the Holy Spirit and leave the results to God. "For we are unto God a sweet savour of Christ, in them that are saved, and in them that perish" (2 Corinthians 2:15).

Spurgeon asserts, "An ambassador is not responsible for the failure of his embassy of peace, nor a fisherman for the quantity of fish he catches, nor a sower for the harvest, but only for the faithful discharge of their respective duties. So the gospel minister [and all His people] is only responsible for the faithful delivery of his message, for the due lowering of the gospel net, for the industrious sowing of the gospel seed."[132]

2. The knowledge of the how of soulwinning thwarts the fear of ineptitude. Confidence in knowing how to present a witness either erases or eases the anxiety of ineptness. See Chapter 4, *The Soulwinners' Training*.

3. The fear of mistakes in soulwinning is thwarted by practice and experience. Thomas Edison had extreme difficulty perfecting the

sound of the phonograph. He would speak the word *specia* into the machine, and it would answer *pecia.* He worked on that problem eighteen hours a day for seven months until it was resolved. If Edison worked that hard on developing the sound of the phonograph, how much more ought believers to work on their witness? Practice, rehearse, study, and practice how to tell a person of Christ until the sound is "perfected." The best way to overcome the fear of witnessing is to practice it. Charles Trumbull said, "There can be no mistake so bad, in working for an individual soul for Christ, as the fatal mistake of not making an honest endeavor."

Think of Edward Kimball. With a burden to win all of his Sunday school class to Christ, he sought to win Dwight Moody. On April 21, 1855, Kimball visited the Holton Shoe Store and found Moody in a stockroom. "I put my hand on his shoulder, and as I leaned over, I placed my foot upon a shoe box. I asked him to come to Christ." To Kimball, it didn't seem to go very well. Moody, however, was gloriously saved and, in time, became the most prominent evangelist in America in the 19th century. The story's moral is that God uses botched and feeble witnessing presentations to win the lost. When soulwinning is done in the deepest sincerity and concern for the lost, mistakes and blunders are rarely noticed by them.

4. Having a witnessing partner thwarts the fear of cowardice in soulwinning. God gave the cowardly Moses a courageous Aaron (Exodus 4:14–16). Through teamwork, they confronted Pharoah effectively. Solomon wisely said, "Two people are better off than one, for they can help each other succeed. If one person falls, the other can reach out and help...A person standing alone can be attacked and defeated, but two can stand back-to-back and conquer" (Ecclesiastes 4:9–10, 12 NLT). The boldness of one infuses courage into the other.

5. The fear of "I can't" in soulwinning is thwarted by dependence upon God, who can. Oswald Chambers asserts, "When it's a question of God's almighty Spirit, never say 'I can't.' If Jesus ever commanded us to do something that He was unable to equip us to accomplish, He would be a liar."[133] God is constantly taking the weak vessels of this world to win souls to showcase His glory and

power (Revelation 3:8). "God stands in need," D. L. Moody said, "not of our strength or wisdom, but of our ignorance, of our weakness; let us but give these to Him, and He can make use of us in winning souls."[134]

"There are many," writes E. Y. Mullins, "who doubt their ability to do successful personal work for Christ. They have an idea that some extraordinary gifts are required, or else they feel that extraordinary attainments are necessary. They imagine that only the highly educated and the specially trained can ever be fitted for such work. Of course, it is true that the greater the education and the more thorough the preparation, other things being equal, the better fitted one will become to do this work, but any Christian with ordinary education [can do it]."[135] Luther said, "God uses crooked sticks to draw straight lines." God works through imperfect and flawed people to bring about His purpose.

6. The fear of initiating a spiritual conversation in soulwinning is thwarted by mastering several approaches. Memorize an approach question or sentence for easy recall to jumpstart the witness. See Chapter 9, *The Soulwinners' Approach.*

7. The fear of insufficient knowledge of the Scriptures in soulwinning is thwarted by biblical study. "A wise person is hungry for knowledge" (Proverbs 15:14 NLT). Knowledge of God's Word increases confidence and infuses peace (quiets anxiety) in soulwinning. "Study to shew thyself approved unto God, a workman that needeth not to be ashamed, rightly dividing the word of truth" (2 Timothy 2:15). David found courage and confidence in the scriptures.[136] "So shall I have wherewith to answer him that reproacheth me: for I trust in thy word" (Psalm 119:42).

8. The fear of not being the type of Christian to do soulwinning is thwarted by God's use of all kinds of people to win souls in the Biblical record.[137] A deacon won the Ethiopian eunuch. Timothy's mother and grandmother won him. Ruth's mother-in-law won her. Peter was won by his brother. A fisherman won Cornelius. Two prisoners won the Philippian jailer. Luke likely was won by a patient (Paul). Many people in Samaria were won by a woman who was a social outcast.

Andrew Murray says, "There exist in a man unsuspected powers which must be called out by training before they are known to be there. When a man thus becomes conscious and master of the power there is in himself, he is, as it were, a new creature; the power and enjoyment of life is doubled. Every believer has hidden within himself the power of saving souls."[138]

*The bottom line.* There is no reason to fear soulwinning, for it's done under God's authority (Matthew 28:18–19), in His power (Acts 1:8), and with His protection (Isaiah 41:10). That which the Lord said to Paul, He says to all: "Do not be afraid; keep on speaking, do not be silent" (Acts 18:9 NIV). "What shall we then say to these things? If God be for us, who can be against us?" (Romans 8:31).

Says Roland Q. Leavell, "When fear torments, the soulwinner should breathe a prayer for courage and faith and love. When afraid to appeal to the lost man in the name of the Savior, the soulwinner should ask for divine daring."[139] "And whatsoever ye shall ask in my name, that will I do, that the Father may be glorified in the Son" (John 14:13). Note that a significant antidote to soulwinning phobia is soulwinning itself.

# 12

# The Soulwinners' Difficulties

Excuses are obstacles to a sinner's conversion that are used to justify and sanction unbelief, rebellious behavior, and delay in salvation. The soulwinner must deftly remove them to bring the person to faith. Note that legitimate, honest excuses must be addressed, not insincere ones. "Do not throw your pearls before swine" (Matthew 7:6 LSB).

Don't despair; there are only a few of these common, age-old excuses, and appropriate Scripture verses can shatter them. Soulwinners may find it helpful to copy the following excuses and their scriptural rebuttal in the flyleaf of their soulwinning New Testaments for easy access.

## 1. *"I Am Waiting on God's Time"*

Many people erroneously believe that God has a specific time for saving people and that they must wait until that moment arrives.[140] Clarify that such is not the case. Tell the person who voices the excuse that the present moment is God's time for their conversion. "Behold, now is the accepted time" (2 Corinthians 6:2).

## 2. *"There Are Many Paths to God"*

Respond to this excuse: "Show me where that is stated in the Bible." They cannot. The Bible clearly states that Jesus Christ is the only path to God and Heaven (John 10:9; Acts 4:12; John 14:6).

## 3. *"I Have Already Been Baptized"*

Reveal to them that baptism is not synonymous with salvation (Acts 8:9–20). Point out that Simon Magus, though baptized by Phillip, was lost. Baptism is a fruit of salvation, not the root (Acts 2:38).

## 4. *"I Need to Straighten My Life Out First"*

Ask, "Can the Ethiopian change his skin, or the leopard his spots?" (Jeremiah 13:23). As a man cannot change his skin color and the leopard cannot change its spots, he likewise cannot straighten out his own life. A sinful nature prevents it. Spurgeon said, "The Ethiopian can wash or paint, but he cannot change that which is part and parcel of himself. A sinner cannot change his own nature."[141] Therefore, waiting until one becomes a better person is futile. The sinner must come to Christ just as he is with his full baggage of sin.

## 5. *"I Am As Good As Those Who Go to Church"*

R. A. Torrey says, "When a person raises this difficulty, you can say, 'So you are troubled about the sins of Christians. Let me show you from God's Word what He says about that.' Then have him read Romans 14:12. Ask, 'Whom does God say you will have to give an account of?'

'Myself.'

'Not of inconsistent Christians, then?'

'No.'

'Are you ready to give an account of yourself to God?'"

Tell them they must stand alone on their record, not another's, at the judgment. Urge the person not to allow the hypocrisy of some Christians to prevent their coming to Christ.

### 6. *"But I'm a Member of the Church"*

Membership in the church is no guarantee of a person's salvation. Point out that attending church is admirable but not synonymous with being a Christian. Nicodemus was avid in church attendance, yet Jesus said unto him, "Ye must be born again" (John 3:7). Tell them that if merely belonging to a church could save, then Jesus' death on the Cross was meaningless.

### 7. *"I Cannot Live the Christian Life"*

Clarify that in salvation it is not their holding on to God that prevails, but rather God's holding on to them, and that His hand will never loosen its grip (John 10:28–29). God enables the worst and weakest sinners who come to Christ to live righteous lives (1 Peter 1:5).

### 8. *"Not Now; Later, I Will Do It"*

Tell the sinner the deadly perils of delay, and thus, the need to be saved immediately.

The peril of death. "Boast not thyself of tomorrow; for thou knowest not what a day may bring forth" (Proverbs 27:1).

The peril of drifting further from Christ and the hardening of the heart toward Him (Hebrews 3:7–8).

The peril of God's wrath. "He, that being often reproved hardeneth his neck, shall suddenly be destroyed, and that without remedy" (Proverbs 29:1). "It is a fearful thing to fall into the hands of the living God" (Hebrews 10:31).

The peril of seeking Christ too late. Have the person read Isaiah 55:6. Then ask him when he is to seek the Lord. Upon the reply "While He may be found," ask when that is. Emphasize that the only time he can be sure of finding Christ is now (2 Corinthians 6:2). Scarborough says, "Urge him to seek God now, for His promises to the sinner are all in the present tense."[142] Oh, the sorrow of coming to Christ one day too late!

## 9. "*I Tried to Be a Christian Before and Failed*"

Ask why he failed. Was it due to a captivating sin or neglect of prayer, Bible study, worship, or service? Or was it due to a religious experience, rather than a spiritual encounter with Christ, which was equated with salvation? If the former, say, "I can show you how to try and not fail." Refer him to Scripture assurances of strength and power to live the Christian life (2 Corinthians 12:9; Philippians 4:13) and invite him to repent (1 John 1:9). Emphasize the imperative of prayer, worship, work, and the Word to stand firm. If the latter is true, urge him to say no to the former experience of mere religion and say yes to genuine salvation (2 Corinthians 13:5).

## 10. "*I Am Too Bad a Person to Be Saved*"

Explain to him that God saved Paul, the chief of sinners (1 Timothy 1:15); the thief on the cross (Luke 23:39–43); the adulterous woman at Jacob's well (John 4); the wicked King Manasseh (2 Chronicles 33:1–21). Point out from the Bible that no person is beyond God's forgiving grace and mercy. "He is able to save completely all who come to God through him" (Hebrews 7:25 TLB). "Whoever comes to me I will certainly not turn away" (John 6:37 CJB). "The Lord says, 'Now, let's settle the matter. You are stained red with sin, but I will wash you as clean as snow. Although your stains are deep red, you will be as white as wool'" (Isaiah 1:18 GNT).

"We have a glorious testimony in the case of Manasseh," says John R. McDuff, "that no sinner need despair. Manasseh is now stooping over the walls of Heaven in company with Saul the blasphemer, Zacchaeus the extortioner, the Magdalene of the Pharisee's house, the dying felon of Calvary, and proclaiming that for the vilest sinner there is mercy. Yes, although this man had defied his God, had scorned pious counsels, had added bloodshed and cruelty to rampant unbelief and lawless lust, yet when the blast of God's trumpet sounded over the apparently impregnable citadel of his heart, it fell to the dust; and from that hour in which grace triumphed, its walls became 'salvation and its gates praise.' And that grace which saved Manasseh can save every one of us—the poorest, the vilest, the most desponding."[143]

> Oh, make but a trial of His love;
>     Experience will decide.
> How bless'd are they—and only they—
>     Who in His truth confide.
>
> ~Tate and Brady (1669)

11. *"I am waiting on the feeling."*

Inquire about the feeling they are waiting for. In most cases, it's a Damascus Road (a blinding light from Heaven) or a Philippian jailhouse (earth-shaking) type. Point out that the only feeling necessary to be saved is that of conviction and sorrow of sin and the desire to turn from it to Christ (John 1:12). If he will open the door to Christ that way, Christ promises to enter and save him (Revelation 3:20) regardless of the absence of blinding lights, earthquakes, or the spiritual upheaval of the heart. Note that multitudes have died and gone to Hell, awaiting an unnecessary feeling that never came.

# 13

# The Soulwinners' Follow-up

The follow-up curriculum? Not theories, philosophies, and opinions, but "whatsoever I have commanded you" (Matthew 28:20). That covers the whole of the Bible— biblical doctrines, disciplines, and duties. Charles Riggs states, "Follow-up is the process through which we establish and equip new believers with the basics of Christianity so they can progress to spiritual maturity and become spiritual reproducers."[144]

Scarborough said, "The evangelism that stops at conversion and public profession is lopsided, wasteful, and incomplete. It should go on to teach, to train, and to develop, and utilize the talents and powers of the new convert. This educational phase of evangelism is transcendently important."[145]  Dawson Trotman wrote, "You can lead a soul to Christ in anywhere from twenty minutes to a couple of hours, but it takes from twenty weeks to a couple of years to get him on the road to maturity."[146]

When should follow-up commence? Immediately. E. Y. Mullins states, "The first days and weeks are most plastic and filled with the greatest possibilities. The first three weeks are worth more than the second three months."[147]

*Care for the Newborn Babes in Christ*

1. Tell him to read the Bible and pray.

Spiritual growth depends upon a daily intake of the Word (Acts 17:11) and time spent in prayer (Ephesians 6:18). Provide the new believer with a copy of the Bible and simple instructions about prayer.

2. Tell him to share the news of his new birth.

Andrew, once saved, told Simon (John 1:41). "If a believer in Christ did not preach in his first two years of his conversion," says Watchman Nee, "he may not likely open his mouth again to preach."

3. Tell him to be baptized.

The eunuch, upon being saved, was immediately baptized, as was the Philippian jailer. "Baptizing [*baptizo*— to immerse] them in the name of the Father, the Son, and the Holy Spirit." All that are saved must be inducted and rooted into the church (membership) through the ordinance of New Testament baptism (immersion in water to profess faith in the death, burial, and resurrection of Jesus for the remission of sins and one's love and allegiance to Him). Christ wants His people to be bound together in close-knit church fellowship, worship, and work.

The Bible states of respondents to Peter's sermon at Pentecost, "Then they that gladly received his word were baptized: and the same day there were added unto them about three thousand souls. And they continued steadfastly in the apostles' doctrine and fellow-ship, and in breaking of bread, and in prayers" (Acts 2:41–42).

Tell him that Jesus deemed the ordinance of baptism important enough that He walked eighty miles to be baptized in the river Jordan by John the Baptist. And Peter says, "It was to this that God called you, for Christ himself suffered for you and left you an example, so that you would follow in his steps" (1 Peter 2:21 GNT). There is only one valid baptism—that which follows conversion to Christ.

4. Tell him to unite with a New Testament Church.

Encourage church affiliation to engage in corporate worship, Christian fellowship, and spiritual service, and to gain instruction and encouragement in living the Christian life (Hebrews 10:25). In and through the varied evangelistic and missionary ministries of the church, the believer can make a difference for eternity in the lives of others locally and even globally by giving financially, witnessing, praying, and serving in various capacities (Romans 12:1).

5. Tell him the importance of the confession of Christ.

"Whosoever therefore shall confess me before men, him will I confess also before my Father which is in heaven" (Matthew 10:32). Peter confessed Jesus to be the Christ, the Son of the Living God (Matthew 16:16). Nathanael confessed, "You are the Son of God! You are the King of Israel!" (John 1:49 ESV). Martha confessed, "I believe that You are the Christ, the Son of God" (John 11:27 NCV). Thomas confessed, saying, "My LORD and my God" (John 20:28).

Christian confession is necessary for four reasons.

*To receive Christ* (as he has done). Without the confession that Jesus is Lord (Savior, ruler, Master), there is no resultant salvation (Romans 10:9).

*To reveal Christ.* In confession, the saint declares the deity of Christ that certifies and authenticates His mission to save man from their sins. Hear Paul's confession of Christ: "Christ was revealed in a human body and vindicated by the Spirit. He was seen by angels and announced to the nations. He was believed in throughout the world and taken to heaven in glory" (1 Timothy 3:16 NLT). Second, he reveals the acceptance of Christ as Lord and Savior. Sincere confession declares one's salvation to the world (1 John 4:2; Matthew 10:32).

*To revere Christ.* Failure to confess Christ openly and boldly, as Peter failed thrice, is to dethrone and disown Him. The Christian is to exalt, honor, and reverence Christ by the confession of life and lip to show that He is Lord. Matthew Henry states, "It is our duty, not only to believe in Christ but to profess that faith. We must never be ashamed of our relation to Christ, our attendance on Him, and our expectations from Him: hereby the sincerity of our faith is evidenced, His name glorified, and others edified."[148]

*To resemble Christ.* Paul writes that when Jesus Christ stood before Pontius Pilate, He "witnessed a good confession" (1 Timothy 6:13). When Pilate asked, "Are You the King of the Jews?" He answered him, saying, "It is as you say." (Luke 23:3 NKJV). Even in the threat of torturous death, Jesus didn't walk back His confession.

6. Enroll him in a new believers' study course on Christian Basics.

Provide instruction in the foundational tenets of the faith, beliefs, and practice through classroom interaction or personal mentoring. My books *Christian Basics 101* and *Growing in Knowledge, Living by Faith* are excellent resources for such a purpose.

7. Be gentle with him. Advises Spurgeon, "Do not throw cold water upon young desires; do not snuff out young believers with hard questions. When they are babes and need the milk of the Word, do not be choking them with your strong meat; they will eat strong meat by and by, but not just yet."[149] See 1 Peter 2:2.

8. Take him soulwinning. Train him to be a skilled soulwinner.

*Helping the convert gain assurance*

The instant a person invites Christ into his life (through repentance and faith), Jesus' work of reconciliation and regeneration occurs. Whereas sincerity of heart must accompany salvation, feelings may or may not. No one is saved, nor is assurance of salvation gained by feeling a certain way. Feelings are not proof of salvation. A person is not to *feel* salvation but *faith* salvation.

The evidence of salvation rests upon God's Word, which loudly states, "To all who received him, he gave the right to become children of God. All they needed to do was to trust him to save them" (John 1:12 TLB). While the believer certainly should feel tremendous gratitude to God and relief that things are eternally settled with Him, validating salvation by emotional experiences is not biblical (Romans 8:16).

Fact, faith, and feeling are like a steam locomotive train. Biblical Fact is the engine that pulls the train, Faith is the boiler that fuels the engine, and Feeling is the caboose. The train must have an engine and a boiler to function, but the caboose is optional.

# 14
# The Soulwinners' Tips

This chapter shares 175 practical tips about effective witnessing and soulwinning. Don't stagger or be discouraged by the number. The amount is necessary to cover the broad spectrum of witnessing/soulwinning in capsule form. They are simple to understand and easy to apply.

1. Be polite. Witness graciously despite the incivility and disrespect received (Luke 10:5, 10). Solomon states, "A soft answer turneth away wrath: but grievous [sharp] words stir up anger" (Proverbs 15:1). Paul said, "Let your speech be always with grace, seasoned with salt, that ye may know how ye ought to answer every man" (Colossians 4:6). Don't yield to rudeness.

Gideon's answer to the men of Ephraim illustrates how a "soft answer" quells anger (Judges 8:1–3). Jephthah's reply to the same tribe pictures the opposite (Judges 12:1–6). William Gurnall said, "Sinners are not pelted into Christ with stones of hard, provoking language, but wooed into Christ by heart-melting exhortations." Remember, it's soulwinning, not *soul-antagonizing*.[150]

He drew a circle that shut me out—
Heretic, rebel, a thing to flout.
But Love and I had the wit to win;
We drew a circle that took him in!
~Edwin Markham (1852–1940)

2. Exhibit humility. Don't be pompous, displaying a holier-than-thou attitude. Smugness repels the lost. "Always be humble and

gentle" (Ephesians 4:2 ERV). Chambers asserts, "When you come to personal dealings with others, remember who you are—you are not some special being created in Heaven, but a sinner saved by grace."[151] Freddie Gage said, "In witnessing, we never approach the lost with the 'BIG ME—little you' attitude. We must maintain a 'little us—GREAT SAVIOR' attitude. Never make a person feel inferior to you."[152]

3. Avoid a condemnatory attitude. J. W. Ellis wrote, "Christ was gentle and kind. Anyone can throw a rock, but it takes wisdom to win souls."[153] Listen without judgment. A Barna survey (2019) revealed that 62 percent of non-Christians favored conversations about the faith with people who "listen without judgment."

4. Don't be pushy. Decisions must not be man-manufactured or manipulated, but Holy Ghost wrought. "A man convinced against his will is unconvinced still." Be persuasive, not pushy. Some fruit is ripe for harvest; others are yet green, requiring further fertilization before plucking. Don't pick unripe fruit. There is no account of any Christian witness in the New Testament "having pushed and pulled or teased and threatened in the effort to get someone to decide for Christ."[154] Remember, it's "not by might, nor by power, but by my Spirit, saith the Lord" (Zechariah 4:6).

5. Keep the witness solemn. Avoid the impression of insincerity. Finney said, "Levity will produce anything but the right impression. You ought to feel that you are engaged in very serious work which is going to affect the character of your friend or neighbor and probably determine his destiny of eternity."[155] Spurgeon says, "I implore you to speak from your hearts or else don't speak at all."[156] He continues, "You may repeat the most affectionate exhortations in such a half-hearted manner that no one will be moved either by love or fear. I believe that for soulwinning, there is more in this matter of earnestness than in almost anything else."

6. Apply the Law of God in the soulwinning message. Failure in the harvest is not due to the Spirit, prepared worker, or the gospel seed, but the unready soil in man's heart. The disposition of the soil determines its readiness and receptivity to the seed (Matthew 13:1–8).

"Break up your fallow ground [unplowed, uncultivated field], and sow not among thorns" (Jeremiah 4:3).

Sowing the gospel seed in bad soil (a heart strewn with the thorns of worldliness, moral corruption, indifference, rebellion toward God, false theology) results in it being disregarded or scorned. The soul must first have its hard, crusty soil broken up by the plow of the law of God (the Ten Commandments) and watering of prayer. Until it is, the ground will remain indifferent and hard as concrete.

John Wesley said, "It is absurd to offer a physician to them that are whole or that at least imagine themselves so to be. You are first to convince them that they are sick; otherwise, they will not thank you for your labor. It is equally absurd to offer Christ to them whose heart is whole, having never yet been broken [by the law]."[157]

G. Campbell Morgan asserts, "The trouble with people who are not seeking a Savior and for salvation is that they do not understand the nature of sin. It is the peculiar function of the Law to bring such an understanding to a man's mind and conscience."[158] Spurgeon states, "The law is the needle, and you cannot draw the silken thread of the Gospel through a man's heart unless you first send the needle of the law to make way for it. If men do not understand the law, they will not feel that they are sinners."[159]

Sin must be acknowledged before saving grace will be sought. Breaking hearts crusted with sin may require many gospel encounters interwoven with the Law.

7. Dress nicely and neatly. Appearance or presentability has the power to open or close a door. Be well groomed.

8. Jettison the religious terminology. Ditch the words of Zion. Use words that connect. Put the cookies on the bottom shelf. State the Gospel as clearly and simply as possible.

9. Dodge controversial subjects such as politics. Spurgeon asserts, "If you are going to win people for Christ, always seek to break down everything that would separate. Do you happen to belong to any political party? Do not bring that subject in. You will

not win souls that way; you will be more likely to excite prejudice and opposition."[160]

10. Never presume a person is a Christian. Almost six decades of witnessing have taught me never to assume a person is saved despite his profession, church membership, or baptism. Approach every prospect as a lost sinner in need of Christ.

11. Exhibit caution and discernment in entering a home alone. The evil that permeates society warrants grave prudence in entering a house without a companion. Jesus sent the seventy out two by two for a reason.

12. Never quit the task despite the failure to win some people. Jesus failed to win Judas, the rich young ruler, or the people of Nazareth, but He didn't stop the work. We will not win all, but we can win some, making the effort worthwhile and profitable.

The soulwinner sows expectantly when the soul is receptive to the good seed. At other times, he sows tearfully when the heart exhibits stubbornness and close-mindedness against the truth of the Gospel (Psalm 126:6). Nevertheless, in season (favorable response) and out of season (unfavorable response), the sowing continues. "We have toiled all night, and taken nothing" makes the task discouraging, but at thy word, "I will let down the net" (Luke 5:5). "And when they had this done, they inclosed a great multitude of fishes: and their net brake" (Luke 5:6).

13. You are not responsible for the results. "I have planted, Apollos watered; but God gave the increase. So then neither is he that planteth any thing, neither he that watereth; but God that giveth the increase" (1 Corinthians 3:6–7). Bill Bright said, "Successful witnessing is taking the initiative to share Christ in the power of the Holy Spirit and leaving the results to God."[161]

A. T. Pierson said, "We are not responsible for conversion, but we are responsible for contact. We cannot compel any man to decide for Christ, but we may entreat every man to decide one way or the other. We may so bring others the gospel message that the responsibility is transferred from us to them. God will take care of the results if we do our part."[162] Arthur Archibald says, "No one fails in this work [soulwinning] except the one who does not make the attempt." It's our part to sow the seed in the power of the Spirit; it is God's part to give the increase.

14. Stay alert to divine appointments. God has prearranged divine appointments for Christians to witness to a 'woman at Jacob's well.' Today, that person is a friend at the end of class, a waiter at the restaurant, someone in the apartment or at the game, a person on the bus, or a fellow employee at work. Often, we too, like Jesus, "must...go through Samaria," be detoured, have plans interrupted, and end up where we didn't intend in order to get to that person at the right time to share the message of Christ!

Stay sensitive to such assigned appointments and do whatever is necessary (miss class, skip lunch, arrive late at work) to show up for them, for such an opportunity may not arise again. Chambers says, "God is the Great Engineer, creating circumstances to bring about moments in our lives of divine importance, leading us to divine appointments." Scarborough said, "God holds the reins that guide souls to Him. It is absolutely necessary that you keep in and up with God [through prayer]."[163]

15. Take ample time to share the message. Be unhurried. Torrey said, "One man with whom slow but thorough work has been done, and who at last has been brought out clearly for Christ, is better than a dozen with whom hasty work has been done, who think they have accepted Christ when in reality they have not."[164] Phillip took time to sit in the chariot with the eunuch to ride with him some distance, explaining the plan of salvation, which resulted in the man's immediate conversion and baptism (Acts 8:29–38).

George E. Sweazey says, "SHORT CUTS IN EVANGELISM NEVER WORK. That invariable rule must be learned soon and remembered often! There is no easy way to bring people to the Christian faith. Only those who are willing to do the most important work in the world in a conscientious, painstaking way will have or deserve to have success."[165]

16. Stay on track in the gospel presentation. Resist chasing rabbits that never will be caught. Save the prospects' unrelated questions until the witness presentation is concluded. Control and guide

the conversation, instead of allowing the prospect to do so. When the prospect dominates the conversation, it must be tactfully maneuvered back into the soulwinners' management.

17. Be clean and holy. "Compromising with sin in your life will never bring you far on evangelism road."[166] "Be ye clean, that bear the vessels of the LORD" (Isaiah 52:11). God can use an educated or an uneducated vessel, a trained or untrained vessel to win souls, but He cannot use a dirty vessel. "Let your light so shine before men, that they may see your good works, and glorify your Father which is in heaven" (Matthew 5:16). A bushel basket, to the degree that it encompasses a light, causes its beam to wane and flicker, dampens its luster and radiance, and impedes its purpose. It is even so with the bushel basket of transgression. It negates or suffocates the believers' profession.

18. Know the enemy of souls and be ready to fight him tooth and nail. E. Y. Mullins says, "Over the soul of that man whom you wish to lead to Christ there is an adversary whose intelligence so far surpasses yours that it cannot be mentioned in comparison; whose power transcends yours so far that they ought never to be placed side by side; who has the experience of six thousand years of conflict; who has been in direct and personal conflict with God Himself; who has placed his foot upon the hearts of ten thousand foes; who has brought to naught the physical strength of Samson, the intellectual culture of Solomon, the piety of David, and millions of men and women—the Devil."[167]

19. Consider the *Who, How, When,* and *Where* of witnessing. First, *who* can reach the person most easily? If not you, then who? The renowned evangelist and soul-winner D. L. Moody told a friend, "My dear Lee, I wish you would talk with my cousin Miss Holton. She thinks a good deal of you, and I think you can lead her to Christ."

*How* is the person to be confronted? Is it best to approach him unexpectedly or by appointment?

*When* should the witness take place? The timing of the witness is crucial. Watch for God's timing, then proceed.

*Where* should the witness take place? Is the best place to share Christ with him at home, in the office, in the church, or on an outing together? The place should be free from any possible interruption and one where the person does not feel threatened.[168]

20. Too many Scriptures may jeopardize the witness. As a rule, one or two appropriate verses for each point in the gospel presentation are sufficient. Too many verses (and illustrations) may serve to confuse or unnecessarily overstate what needs to be said. Sometimes, a single text is adequate.

21. Never argue with the prospect. Jesus avoided argument. Don't win an argument, only to lose the soul. "Truth does not need a defender, nor theology an apologist. Many times a quiet, gentle spirit wins where a brainy argument drives away."[169] Said D. L. Moody, "When men argue, I give them the Bible. When they say, 'We don't believe in the Bible,' I just keep right on giving them the Word of God."

22. Avoid distractions. Witness without interruption, interference, or delay. "Salute no man by the way" (Luke 10:4b). Haste is required in witnessing. Souls are perishing. Doors are closing. Opportunities are passing. An UN-DIVIDED (Undivided), UNDEVIATING ATTENTION to the task is necessary. No time is to be lost! The believer must say what His Lord said, "I must work the works of him that sent me, while it is day: the night cometh, when no man can work" (John 9:4).

23. Don't say more than required. Be sensitive to when what is said is enough. A student interrupted a pastor's sharing of a lengthy booklet on how to be saved, stating, "Do I have to hear all that before I get saved." The pastor stopped the presentation, and the youth immediately prayed to receive Christ.

How much ought the soulwinner to share? It depends on the prospect's spiritual state—his knowledge, understanding, and soul condition. It may take a few quick steps, as with Zacchaeus (Luke 19:5–9), or many, as with the Samaritan woman at Jacob's well (John 4:7–42). Therefore, sensitivity to the person's readiness (cultivated or uncultivated soil) determines the extent and depth of the gospel presentation. Don't overload the lost with information.

Too much, too soon, complicates. Duryea forcibly said, "The sick soul needs not a lecture on medicine, but a prescription."[170]

24. Be skilled in several evangelistic methods. Be ready to change the approach on a dime due to interruptions, time constraints, language and cultural barriers. Henry Ward Beecher said the soulwinner must "adapt his instruments according to their [the sinners] peculiarities—providing a spear for some, a hook for others, a net for others, and baits for each one, as each one will."[171]

25. Exhibit patience. "And let us not be weary in well doing: for in due season we shall reap, if we faint not" (Galatians 6:9). Any fisherman will tell you that fishing requires patience and perseverance. The same is true with fishing for souls. Jeremiah attests that he witnessed (fished) for ten long years without winning a soul (Jeremiah 25:3).

26. Develop a ten- to twenty-second "elevator" witness. A gospel presentation compacted into a few sentences will be handy on elevators, at check-out counters, restaurants, and foxholes in battle.

27. Be tactful. Tact is finesse and sensitivity in confronting the lost. It's saying and doing the right thing at the right time. Jesus, in His approach to the woman at Jacob's well, did not immediately say, "Lady, you need to be saved." He took time to ask her for a drink of water before proceeding with the witness (John 4:9–10). Phillip tactfully approached the Ethiopian eunuch, asking, "Understandest thou what thou readest?" (Acts 8:30).

28. Use a marked New Testament, not the whole Bible. Take your pistol (New Testament), not your shotgun (Study Bible), on soulwinning visitation. This is done not out of shame for the Bible but to enhance receptivity to the visit.

29. Designate who the talker (presenter of the Gospel) and silent partner (distraction handler, babysitter) will be before entering the home.

30. Practice oral hygiene. Carry breath mints.

31. Don't speak ill of a fellow worker or church. Remember, the purpose of the soulwinning visit is to win a soul to Christ, not badger other churches or ministers.

32. Don't discount the supernatural change set in motion (domino effect) when a soul is saved (2 Corinthians 5:17). Immanuel Kant states that every personality is like a pyramid resting on its apex.[172] One choice, a decision for Christ, can alter that apex and impact the entire structure (domino effect) of the personality forever (happiness, purpose, hope, career, marriage, eternity).

33. Assess the prospect. Jon Courson says, "To be effective in ministry, we must make judgments—not for condemnation, but for identification. Is this person open? Is he sensitive? Is he hungering? Or does he just want to argue and discuss endlessly? The Lord loves to see us effective, and Satan would love to see us sidetracked."[173]

34. Don't overstay the visit. Keep the door open for future visits. "Never worry the unsaved with long, over-pressed appeal. When you see they are irritated or bored or restless or angered, leave them and seek again to reach them."[174]

35. The lost often are easily offended and insulted. Tread gently and tactfully.

36. Exhibit expectation. "He that ploweth should plow in hope" (1 Corinthians 9:10). Pessimism impedes the task. "Expect great things from God. Attempt great things for God." "But without faith it is impossible to please him" (Hebrews 11:6). "And when He was come into the house, the blind men came to Him: and Jesus saith unto them, Believe ye that I am able to do this? They said unto Him, Yea, Lord" (Matthew 9:28). Saith Spurgeon, "The most likely instrument to do the Lord's work is the man who expects God will use him and who goes forth to labor in the strength of that conviction."[175]

37. Keep records of souls won. An accurate report of the number of souls won benefits the church. To hear the word of souls being snatched as brands from the burning encourages saints to engage in the work. Spurgeon states, "It is by no means an evil thing for workers to be encouraged by having some account of results before them."[176] But he cautions, "Do not number your fish before they are broiled or count your converts before you have tested and tried them."[177] The broadcasting of statistics becomes wrong when done boastfully, haughtily, or in fleshly competition with another.

38. Always be ready to share. "Be instant in season, out of season" (2 Timothy 4:2). John R. Rice says, "The best soulwinners are those who go when it is convenient and then go when it is not convenient." Faris Whitesell said, "There are no eight-hour days and forty-hour weeks in this work of reaping the harvest."[178]

Paul was always ready to share the Gospel. He was prepared to witness the Gospel at the riverside to Lydia, in a jailhouse to a chief jailer, in a courthouse to King Agrippa, in leg irons to his Roman guards in Rome, to a fortune teller in Philippi, to the household of the Philippian jailer at midnight. This man refused to be silenced. Despite the cost or consequence, he was always ready to speak of the Savior who saved him.

39. Be associated with a local New Testament church. Spurgeon said, "Christian laborers disconnected from the Church are like sowing and reaping without having any barn to store the fruits of the harvest; they are useful but incomplete."[179] The church is the only ordained hub of missionary endeavors. Faris Whitsell asserts, "Personal evangelism is at its best when operating in and through the New Testament local church."[180]

40. Invite the lost sinner to church to hear the Gospel.

41. Take a pad and pen to record information about the visit that may be helpful for future contact. "The palest ink is better than the best memory."

42. Don't allow decisions that are not genuine to discourage you from new efforts. The sower will encounter four responses (Matthew 13:19–23).

*The unknowledgeable hearer*. The hearer impulsively receives the Word but without understanding.

*The momentary hearer*. The Word joyfully is received but fails to take root in the soul.

*The worldly-minded hearer*. The cares and concerns of the world suffocate the Word in the hearer before it takes root.

*The sincere hearer*. With understanding, the hearer receives, retains, professes, and practices it. The sower and the seed were the same in this case as in the others; the difference was the readiness of the soil. Superficial professions will happen, despite conscientious efforts to avoid them, but they ought not to discourage soulwinning.

43. Plead for soulwinning wisdom. Do you feel inapt to witness? Trust God to give insight into doing it. "If any of you lack wisdom, let him ask of God, who giveth to all men liberally...and it shall be given him"? (James 1:5 KJ21). Matthew Henry asserts, "Those that would win souls have need of wisdom to know how to deal with them, and those that do win souls show that they are wise."[181] Samuel Chadwick said, "We need wisdom beyond our own to win the souls of men, and the power that is also of God. For myself, I covet above all gifts the power of wisdom to win souls for my Lord."

44. Focus on winning just one soul (at the start). Moody said, "If you win only one soul to Christ, you may set a stream in motion that will flow long after you are dead and gone. So if you turn one to Christ, that one may turn a hundred; they may turn a thousand, and so the stream, small at first, goes on broadening and deepening as it rolls toward eternity."[182]

Don't dismiss the value of winning just one to Christ. R. G. Lee remarked, "One may be many. Andrew brought Simon—just one. But that one won many, for under God, Simon brought 3,000 in one day. Jack Stratton, a waiter in a restaurant, brought John Gough to Christ—just one. And Gough brought many to Christ. A Sunday school teacher, Edward Kimball, brought Moody to Christ—just one. But that one won many, for Moody reached two continents for God. But why say more? Just as one digit is valuable in the multiplication table and one letter in the alphabet, far more valuable is just one soul in God's sight."[183] Keble said, "The salvation of one soul is worth more than the framing of a Magna Charta of a thousand worlds."

45. Never interrupt another soulwinner's presentation. Don't interfere with another's witness nor allow them to interfere with yours. If possible, the soulwinning partner must not speak and must protect his partner from being interrupted. If, as the silent partner, you are talked to by another family member, reply courteously and briefly and turn the attention back to your companion presenting the Gospel.

46. Win the children. "Suffer little children…to come unto me" (Matthew 19:14). The field whitest unto harvest ready for reaping is that of children. Sixty-three percent of individuals who become Christians do so between the ages of 4 and 14.[184] Use words that connect. Keep the presentation short. Stick to the most elementary principles. Employ a simple method, like that of the Wordless Book. Note that Spurgeon used the Wordless Book, one of colors, to explain salvation in the sermon "The Wordless Book" on January 11, 1866. The book is credited to his authorship. Saith Scarborough, "The saving of a child's soul offers a double opportunity; that is, to save a soul from eternal destruction and to develop a life and talents for the service of God."

47. Witnessing should become spontaneous. Richard Halverson said, "New Testament Christians did not witness because they had to but because they could not help it."[185] Witnessing should be so commonplace to the believer that it happens intuitively. "For we cannot but speak the things which we have seen and heard" (Acts 4:20).

48. Pray for laborers for the harvest. "The harvest truly is plenteous, but the laborers are few. Pray ye, therefore, the Lord of the harvest, that He will send forth laborers into His harvest" (Matthew 9:37–38). This text haunted Spurgeon more than any other. There is a shortage of workers in the harvest.

There is a labor shortage despite the precept that every believer is to do the work (Matthew 28:18–20). Though every Christian is commanded to win souls, scarcely five percent obey. There is a labor shortage despite the power given for the work (Acts 1:8). There is a labor shortage despite a partnership with Christ in the work (1 Corinthians 3:9). There is a labor shortage despite the peril of the lost sinner in need of the work (Revelation 21:8). There is a labor shortage despite the pay provided for the work (Daniel 12:3; Job 36:11; Matthew 19:29).[186] The solution to the problem is "pray ye" for laborers to be raised up and thrust out into the vast mission field.

"The real need," says Bailey Smith, "is not to pray for souls but soulwinners."[187] He explains, "The most effective praying is not for the lost world but rather for the saved to have a concern for the world that's lost. Prayer then is to be used to get the saved awakened to the lostness of the lost."[188]

What kind of laborers are we to pray to be supplied? Spurgeon answers, "We need laborers, not loiterers. We need men on fire. The harvest can never be reaped by men who will not labor—they must be off with their coats and go at it in their shirtsleeves. I mean, they must doff their dignities and get to Christ's work as if they meant it, like real harvest men."[189] Set your watch or cell phone to alarm at 9:38 a.m. (Matthew 9:38) daily to prompt prayer for more laborers in the harvest.

49. Cultivate connections with prospects. Keep a list of the names of those who are interested in but as yet unresponsive to the Gospel. Cultivate them through displays of interest and concern—visits, cards, phone calls, and emails.

50. Be bold as a lion. "The wicked flee when no man pursueth: but the righteous are bold as a lion" (Proverbs 28:1). Display a boldness in witnessing like that of John Vassar, who, upon meeting President Grant, held to his hand until he had told him of Christ and courteously questioned his salvation.

Gregory said, "The lion is not afraid in the onset of beasts because he knows well that he is stronger than them all. Whence the fearlessness of a righteous man is rightly compared to a lion, because, when he beholds any rising against him, he returns to the confidence of his mind and knows that he overcomes all his adversaries because he loves Him alone whom he cannot in any way lose against his will."[184] An African proverb says, "The lion does not turn around when a small dog barks."

The Bible says that when Jesus approached the cross accompanied by the disciples, "As they (disciples) followed, they were afraid" (Mark 10:32). To the disciples' credit, fear of the unknown did not stagger their faith in Christ, weaken their allegiance to Christ, or impede their mission for Christ. Despite being afraid, they remained confident and courageous. In that, they are worthy examples to imitate.

Mark Twain said, "Courage is resistance to fear, mastery of fear, not absence of fear." Courage amid fear must be exhibited in soulwinning. Paul says, "For God hath not given us the spirit of fear; but of power, and of love, and of a sound mind" (2 Timothy 1:7). Martin Luther King, Jr., said, "We must constantly build dikes of courage to hold back the flood of fear." See Acts 4:17–20.

51. Primary bridges to faith are friends and relatives. Elmer Towns states that 86 percent of Christians testify that friends and relatives influenced their decision to be saved.[190] Application: Empower friendship networks and family relationships as bridges to share the Gospel.

52. Keep outreach efforts above board, ethical, and honest. Don't use the bait-and-switch methods of the world in the King's business. Employ every *honorable* means to spread the Gospel, including personal evangelism, evangelistic preaching, tract distribution, radio and television, the internet, and evangelistic events (harvest days, revivals, etc.).

53. Don't let the distribution of tracts take the place of sharing the Gospel verbally.

54. Witnessing encounters sometimes ought to be aborted out of safety concerns. Matthew Henry writes, "In case of great peril, the disciples of Christ may go out of the way of danger, though they must not go out of the way of duty. No sinful, unlawful means may be used to escape [only that open door the Holy Spirit provides]."[191] Plumer states, "It sometimes happens that there is more real heroism in daring to fly from danger than in stopping to meet it. To stop and meet useless risks because one is afraid of being called a coward is one of the subtlest forms of cowardice, and the desire to be thought brave is not a high motive for courageous action."[192] Paul and Barnabas, in discovering a plot in Iconium to stone them, fled the town to escape it (Acts 14:5–7). See Acts 16:6.

Blomberg comments, "Jesus calls His followers to bravery but not foolishness. God's Word can go forth powerfully through the unspoken testimony of martyrdom, but it is often better for people to remain alive to speak it aloud."[193]

55. Nothing can substitute for soulwinning. Adrian Rogers stated, "I care not how faithfully you attend, how eloquently you teach, how liberally you give, how circumspectly you walk, how beautifully you sing; if you are not witnessing, you are not right with God."[194]

56. Aim for an immediate decision. "A true witness delivereth souls" (Proverbs 14:25). Don't doubt the power of God to save a soul instantly. The penitent thief was saved instantly. The jailer was saved instantly. The woman at the well was saved instantly. The eunuch was saved instantly. Expect souls to be saved each time you witness. "It is possible for a life-changing decision to take place during one visit, and often it does."[195] A soul's present and eternal destiny may hinge on the decision of the moment.[196]

57. Witness primarily to people of the same sex as yourself. Men should never put themselves in a place with a woman alone, nor a woman with a man.

58. Think lightly of Hell, and you will think lightly of lost souls. When asked the secret of his soulwinning success, Billy Sunday walked over to a window and, looking upon the masses of people on the street, declared, "They are going to Hell! They are going to Hell! They are going to Hell!" He said, "If there is a secret to my winning so many souls, it is because I really believe that men without Christ are going to Hell."

59. Confront the prospect privately. Privacy with the prospect is crucial. Once a third person enters the picture, the witness is generally impeded and closes down. R. A. Torrey asserts, "No one likes to open his heart freely to another on this most personal and sacred of all subjects when there are others present. Many will, from pride, defend themselves in a false position when several are present, who would fully admit their error or sin or need if they were alone with you."

60. Contact is imperative. While "tact" is important, "contact" is more necessary.[197] "It is the cooping yourselves up in rooms," states Jonathan Edwards, "that has dampened the work of God, which never was and never will be carried out to any purpose without going into the highways and hedges and compelling men and women to

come in."[198] Remember, Jesus sat with sinners and tax collectors (Matthew 9:10). The chance of winning a sinner to Christ is zero if you are never with a sinner. At a crusade, I saw a lady wearing a shirt that read, "The church has left the building. Gone fishing." That says it all.

61. Learn to spell "Go." How do you spell "go"? Do you spell it "pray"? The saint is to pray for the unsaved, but there comes a time when he must leave off praying and begin telling. Says Spurgeon, "Prayer and action must go together. Action without prayer— presumption; prayer without action— hypocrisy."[199]

Do you spell it "giving"? Financially investing in evangelism and missions is tremendously important, something the believer should do, but the Great Commission cannot be obeyed by proxy. Do you spell it "visitation"? Extending a kind invitation to another to attend church is commendable, but it doesn't replace sharing the gospel message. Do you spell it "pastor"? Witnessing is every man's responsibility, not just that of the ministerial staff. Do you spell it "cultivation"? Though often essential, plowing the field must not become a substitute for sowing. Do you spell it "stay"?

"Go" can only be spelled "go." "Go tell it on the mountain, over the hills, and ev'rywhere; go tell it on the mountain that Jesus Christ is born." "Tell the good news, tell the good news, tell the good news to everyone."

William Booth states, "Go for souls. Go straight for souls, and go for the worst." Bailey Smith said, "The other things that we have to do may be called important by those around us, but there is nothing more important to do than to win a person to Jesus Christ."[200]

62. Don't judge or condemn another's style of winning souls. The person instrumental in winning souls (though their methods differ from our own) should be honored and valued, not demeaned (Isaiah 52:7). Jesus said, "For he that is not against us is on our part" (Mark 9:40).

Spurgeon said, "He who actually, really, and truly turns men from the error of their ways to God, and so is made the means of saving them from going down to Hell, is a wise man; and that is true of him whatever his style of soul winning....He may be a Paul, deeply logical, profound in doctrine, able to command all candid judgments...an Apollos, grandly rhetorical, whose lofty genius soars into the very heaven of eloquence...or a Cephas, rough and rugged, using uncouth metaphor and stern declamation; but if he wins souls, he is no less than his polished brother or his argumentative friend, but not else. To their own Master they are accountable for how they work, not to us."[201] Augustine said, "A wooden key is not so beautiful as a golden one, but if it can open the door when the golden one cannot, it is far more useful."

63. Train the ears to hear the prompting of the Spirit. Hearing God's voice is essential in every facet of the Christian life but of immense importance in soulwinning. Had Phillip not heard God speak to him regarding the searching lost sinner traveling the Gaza strip, this man would not have been saved. Had Peter not heard God's voice telling him to witness to Cornelius, Cornelius would never have been saved. These men had trained ears to listen to the voice of God above the voices of all others clamoring for attention.

The believer must discipline himself to learn to hear the still small voice of God, for multiple times in life He will speak with specific soulwinning assignments, saying, "Go here or go there and speak to him or her now." Failure to hear God, when He speaks, will result in failed assignments and lost souls.

64. Do not grieve the Holy Spirit. To grieve the Spirit by disobedience in witnessing is to cause His power to be withdrawn or blocked (Ephesians 4:30). L. J. Ogilvie asserts, "The Lord's power will not be squandered on us for long if we refuse to be channels of His grace as witnesses."[202]

65. Be sound and thorough, void of shallowness. "*Solemnly* testifying to both Jews and Greeks of repentance toward God and faith in our Lord Jesus Christ" (Acts 20:21 NASB). The testifying of Paul stated here was not that of personal experience but the comprehensive declaration of the gospel message couched in the Holy Scriptures (Acts 20:27). Like Paul, the soulwinner must

primarily "declare...all the counsel of God," based on the Scriptures, not just present testimonies based on feelings and experiences.

66. Be sensitive to the working of the Spirit (watch for clues) in a person's life. Henry Blackaby states, "People do not seek God on their own initiative. People don't ask questions about spiritual matters unless God is at work in their lives. When you see someone seeking God or asking questions about Christianity, you are witnessing God at work. That is something that only God does in people's lives."[203]

67. Don't discount your abilities to witness. Alexander Maclaren states, "What does the shape of the cup matter? What does it matter, whether it be gold or clay? The main thing is that it shall bear the water of life to some thirsty lip. All Christians have...to tell the Good News. Their task is to carry a message—no refinement of words is needed for that; arguments are not needed."[204] Moody said, "God stands in no need of our strength or wisdom but of our ignorance, of our weakness; let us but give these to Him, and He can make use of us in winning souls."

68. Don't tell the sinner the XYZs of the Bible; tell him the ABCs. "For some have not the knowledge of God" (1 Corinthians 15:34). "Not the knowledge" means "ignorance, not to be acquainted with something." Zodhiates says, "In the New Testament, it is not merely an intellectual ignorance but a moral defect or fault, a willful ignorance or blindness."[205] This ignorance demands that we treat the oldest of men as the youngest of children in sharing the Gospel.[206] Stick to the foundational and essential biblical truth that makes plain man's spiritual plight and only remedy.

69. Strive for a heart for souls. Professor John Stuart Blackie, who gave up his chair at Edinburgh University to spend the rest of his life winning souls, had a heart for souls. He said, "Let Greek die, let Hebrew die, let learning go to the dogs if need be; but let souls live."

Paul said, "O my Jewish brothers! How I long for you to come to Christ. My heart is heavy within me, and I grieve bitterly day and night because of you. Christ knows and the Holy Spirit knows that it is no mere pretense when I say that I would be willing to be forever damned if that would save you" (Romans 9:1–3 TLB). He possessed a heart for souls.

A heart for souls was possessed by Hamblin, who said, "I feel like a man who has been wrecked at sea and has got into the lifeboat but sees his fellows sinking all about him! I must hurry then, for while I am saving one, others are going down." John Vassar, of whom it was said, "Rest was a stranger to him while souls were around him unsaved,"[207] knew what it was to have a heart for souls.

Spurgeon knew what it was to have such a heart, for he said to the unsaved, "I will try again; and if, unhappily, I should fail again, I will continue at the work as long as you live and I am able to reach you. I cannot endure that you should die in your sins! I will go before God in secret and lay your case before Him and beg Him to interpose. We cannot let you be damned. It is too dreadful. We cannot stand by and see you lost."[208]

George Whitefield, who said, "Give me souls, or take my soul," possessed the heart for souls.

> I want to be a soulwinner
> For Jesus ev'ry day;
> He does so much for me.
>
> I want to aid the lost sinner
> To leave his erring way
> And be from bondage free.
>
> ~J. W. Ferrill (1907)

70. Use decision cards. To affirm the decision, the prospect checks a block on the decision card that reads, "I received Jesus Christ into my life as Lord and Savior and purpose to live for Him all my life." He then records the date and time of the decision in the space provided and signs his name.

71. Don't infringe upon people. No one likes to be late for an appointment or have their meal interrupted.

72. Evaluate the witnessing encounter. Critiquing a witness sharpens it.

73. Upon knocking on the front door, step several steps back to create an unthreatening space between the person and yourself.

74. Recognize the signs (opportunities) to share the Gospel. A man prayed, "Lord, if you want me to witness to someone today, please give me a sign to show me who it is."

Shortly afterward, on an almost empty bus, a tall, burly man sat beside him and, in tears, cried out loudly, "I need Jesus. I am a lost sinner on my way to Hell. I need to be saved. Will you tell me how to become a Christian?"

The man bowed and prayed, "Lord, is this a sign?"[209] Pray for opportunities to share Christ. And identify them when they come.

75. Stay alert for witnessing opportunities following church services. The close of a church service is a great time to speak to a person about the need of Christ. Having pierced the soul and awakened it to the must of salvation, the sermon has prepared someone to be led to Christ. The witness approach may be by way of the question, "What did you think of the sermon?" It is most expedient, however, that a person only be approached if the witness is prompted by the Holy Spirit. If the person manifests resistance, share a warm wish for a good day and depart.

Spurgeon said, "We want, in the Church of Christ, a band of well-trained sharpshooters, who will pick the people out individually and be always on the watch for all who come into the place, not annoying them, but making sure that they do not go away without having had a personal warning, a personal invitation, and a personal exhortation to come to Christ."[210]

76. Redeem the opportunities to share the Gospel before it's too late. The time for influencing and winning souls to Christ is limited. "So then, as we have opportunity, let us work" (Galatians 6:10 ASV). "As long as it is day, we must do the works of him who sent me. Night is coming, when no one can work" (John 9:4 NIV). Matthew Henry says, "The night comes, it will come certainly, may come suddenly, is coming nearer and nearer. When the night comes, we cannot work because the light afforded us to work by is extinguished. And, besides, our time allotted for our work will then

have expired."[211] "The time is long enough for the work but too short to allow trifling."[212] Someone has said, "Opportunity does not come to the person who waits for it, but to the person who makes it." "Make the most of your chances to tell others the Good News. Be wise in all your contacts with them" (Colossians 4:5 TLB).

77. Engage in trotline fishing. Inciting others to fish for souls increases the catch. Vance Havner asserts, "It is better to wake up five hundred Christians than to convert five hundred sinners, for if five hundred Christians wake up, they will win more than five hundred sinners."[213]

78. Rest in the protection of the Lord. Warren Wiersbe said, "The safest place in all the world is in the will of God, and the safest protection in all the world is the name of God." The Scriptures say, "The name of the Lord is a strong tower; the righteous run to it and are protected" (Proverbs 18:10 CSB) and "The Lord keeps you from all harm and watches over your life. The Lord keeps watch over you as you come and go, both now and forever" (Psalm 121:7–8 NLT).

79. Endure rejection and mistreatment. When the risk of temporal rejection and possible scorn from the sinner is weighed against his eternal rejection by God and eternal abode in Hell, we have no option but to go and tell him how to be saved. "Therefore I take pleasure in infirmities, in reproaches, in necessities, in persecutions, in distresses for Christ's sake" (2 Corinthians 12:10).

80. Collect intel about the prospect. Visitation records of the church provide information collected from past visits that will prove beneficial (family, work or school, response to previous visits, interest level, and whether the Gospel was presented or not, etc.).

81. Aim to win souls regardless of circumstance. Andrew Murray said, "Everyone cannot go abroad or give his whole time to direct work, but everyone, whatever his calling or circumstances, can give his whole heart to live for souls and the spread of the kingdom."[214]

82. Write evangelistic books. Evangelistic books bear witness to Christ. The soulwinner's voice and the preacher's cries die out, but a book about Jesus will last centuries. The writings of Spurgeon, who

died in 1892, have allowed him to influence millions for the cause of Christ. E. P. Whipple states, "Books are lighthouses erected in the great sea of time."

83. Reaping is proportionate to the degree of sowing. Paul wrote, "He who soweth sparingly shall reap also sparingly, and he who soweth bountifully shall reap also bountifully" (2 Corinthians 9:6 KJ21). The text refers to the law of stewardship and the harvesting of souls.

84. Disburse the Gospel seed fittingly with just honor and expectation. Believers bear *precious* seed (Psalm 126:6). Spurgeon frankly says, "Tell it out as those who know it is *precious*, not flippantly or as though we were retelling a mere story from the *Arabian Nights*. Tell out the truth as it is in Jesus, with the firm conviction that there is life in it, and something will come of it. Our estimate of the preciousness of the seed will have much to do with the result of the seed."[215]

85. Clarify to the lost sinner the difference between belief and trust. Years ago, Blondin cautiously pushed a wheelbarrow across a tightrope that stretched across the roaring Niagara Falls. The crowd applauded the remarkable feat. He asked, "Who of you believe I can push someone in this wheelbarrow across the falls?" All agreed that he could. Stunningly, he asked, "Who of you is willing to be that person?" There were no takers.

What was believed in their head wasn't trusted in their heart. It is one thing to believe that Jesus can forgive sin and save the soul from the penalty of sin, yet something else to sit down in the wheelbarrow trusting Him to do so. Salvation involves more than head knowledge (mental assent). It takes heart trust.

86. The most effective method is to share with one person at a time. John R. Rice, after seeing tens of thousands come to Christ, said, "I can say that personal contact, personal invitation, has a part in winning nine out of ten of all those I have seen come to Christ. If all the preachers that preach big sermons on 'Ye Must Be Born Again' would use those words to one individual, no doubt many more would be saved." Robert L. Sumner says, "A message that

seems ineffective before a large congregation may result in eternal fruit when presented man to man."[216]

87. The will of God is the main incentive for soulwinning. Faris Whitesell asserts, "The will of God should be the determinate factor in all our activity. We may not be certain what God's will is about some things, but about soulwinning, we can have no doubt. Christ has plainly said that we should be fruitful (John 15:8), that we should make disciples of all nations (Matthew 28:19), and that we should be His witnesses in all places (Acts 1:8)."

88. Provide evidence for the faith when expedient. "But sanctify the Lord God in your hearts: and be ready always to give an answer to every man that asketh you a reason of the hope that is in you with meekness and fear" (1 Peter 3:15). See Chapter 17, "The Soulwinners' Apologetics."

89. Don't be derailed by trivial questions posed during the encounter. The best way to handle nonessential questions is to say, "That's a good question. I will answer it in a moment, but let's finish looking at this passage first." When the presentation is done, ask, "What question did you want me to answer?"

90. Treat the visit as the prospect's one and only. No other soulwinner will likely enter the prospect's home. Make the very best of it. Posted in a parachute factory was a large sign that read, "Make every chute the best possible. It's the pilot's last chance."

91. Leave a gospel tract with the undecided. In the absence of a soulwinner, a tract speaks of how to find the way of salvation.

92. The soulwinner cannot make people respond to Christ. Spurgeon says, "We cannot make the fish bite, but we can do our best to draw them near to the killing bait of the Word of God; and once they are there, we will watch and pray till they are fully taken."[217]

93. Restrict the time spent in a Christian's home. Where visits reveal the person is a faithful Christian and church member, share brief pleasantries, and then press on to other homes. Don't let hours of chit-chat with saints rob you of the valuable time needed to pursue the lost.

94. There is no vacation or retirement from this work. Watchman Nee says, "[Winning souls] is something you cannot outgrow; it is a lifetime undertaking."[218] Exhibit stickability to the task, whatever may come. More than twenty years after Paul's conversion, he said that with the help of God, he continued "witnessing both to small and great" (Acts 26:22). He stood firm, immovable in the job, despite the calamities, persecution, and opposition that assailed him.

95. The soulwinner leading the gospel presentation should sit nearest the prospect.

96. Don't seek decisions but disciples. Ray Comfort advises, "Divorce yourself from the thought that you are merely seeking 'decisions for Christ.' What we are praying for is repentance within the heart."[219]

97. Close the witness as soon as possible, but not too soon.

98. Close a nonproductive visit quickly and with prayer. When discerning disinterest or inattention by the prospect, it's time to close the visit and leave; arise and say, "It's been good to visit with you. Please think about what was shared. We hope you will soon decide for Christ. In the meantime, please come and visit our church. Before we go, I would like to pray for you."

99. Ponder ways to break the ice with the prospect. The use of compliments, pleasantries, connections that someone in the home may have with the church, matters of common interest, and expressions of congratulations for a new job or an accomplishment should all be considered.

100. You don't have to have the answers to all the questions in order to witness (no one does), just the basic ones about the *what, why,* and *how* of salvation, which are quickly learned and easily shared.

101. Stay optimistic. An old man walking on the beach early one morning noticed a young boy picking up starfish and casting them back into the ocean. He inquired about the reason for what he saw. The youth stated he was trying to save the starfish from death. "But

the beach goes on for miles, and there are millions of starfish," countered the man. "How can your effort make a difference?"

The boy picked up a starfish and thrust it as far as he could into the waves, replying, "It makes a difference to this one."

102. Don't feel overwhelmed by methods that others advocate and use. It's not the technique used but the result that counts. Use the method that can be used best. Many soulwinners have found success in using only one verse, like John 3:16, and others in using booklets or plans like the Roman Road. There's no need to complicate and make the gospel presentation difficult.

103. Count the cost to be a soulwinner. Roland Q. Leavell defines the price of being a soulwinner. "Others may walk in the counsel of the ungodly; the soulwinner cannot. Others may pursue worldly pleasure; soulwinners cannot. Others may shirk sacred obligations on Sunday; soulwinners cannot. Others may be casual in church life; soulwinners cannot. Others may be shallow students of the Bible; soulwinners cannot. Others may be dilatory in duty; soulwinners cannot. Others may doubt the necessity of regeneration; soulwinners cannot. Others may look lightly at the sinfulness of sin; soulwinners cannot. Others may be skeptical about Heaven and Hell; soulwinners cannot. Others may love the pre-eminence; soulwinners cannot. Others may demand a display of their virtues and victories; soulwinners cannot. Others may be at ease in Zion; soulwinners cannot."[220] Spurgeon says, "The diver plunges deep to find pearls, and we may accept any labor or hazard to win a soul."[221]

104. The timeline of salvation varies. Some respond immediately, while others require time to resolve their questions and concerns. The winning of a soul may take three or more encounters. Research indicates that, on average, a person hears the Gospel 3.4 times before he accepts Christ. Usually, each time the Gospel is presented, they step closer to deciding for Christ ("The Law of Three Hearings").[222]

105. Teamwork soulwinning is like three links in a chain. At Amsterdam '83, Billy Graham said that soulwinning was like several links in a chain. Link A is the initial contact with a soul about Christ. Link B in the chain is the cultivation of the seed sown in Link A.

Link C draws the net, bringing the soul to a decision for Christ. Effectiveness in soulwinning hinges on understanding at which link the soulwinner is at the time of the encounter.

It's been said that "God never gives any one man a whole soul." W. Y. Fullerton stated, "We must be ready to reap the harvest that has been sown by others and to acknowledge their sowing; we must equally be ready to sow the seed for others to reap. It is a great art to drop a sentence in the midst of a conversation and to pass on without waiting for a response, without demanding an answer or starting a discussion, simply just trusting the seed. The expert in the quest for souls will often be content to plant an acorn without expecting to see the tree grow."[223]

106. Keep the promises made to the prospect (to visit again, provide resources, assist with needs).

107. Engage in soulwinning prayer for the unsaved hearing the evangelistic sermon. A minister dreamed of seeing rows of beautiful diadems studded with stunning jewels. "Is that big one for me?" said he, remembering that many had been saved in his church.

"No, not for you," the angel said. "That one is for the poor, old deaf man who used to sit by your pulpit stairs and plead with God for souls in the congregation while you preached to them." What a change would occur in our churches if more prayed earnestly for souls to be saved as the man of God preached, especially during the invitation!

108. There are three sound barriers in soulwinning, much like an airplane passes in taking off to flight. Each can cause anxiety and uneasiness. The first "sound barrier" is transitioning to the spiritual in conversation (movement from sports or weather to the Gospel). The second "sound barrier" is experienced when asking the person if he or she will receive Christ. Nervousness arises, and you must blast through fears and hesitation. The third "sound barrier" is faced when pressing for a decision for Christ then and there.[224] Perhaps this is the most challenging barrier to blast through, but certainly the most important. With each "sound barrier," the jet propulsion blast of the Holy Spirit is provided to press through it.

109. Don't always take the first no to the invitation to be saved as final. Sometimes, clarification of gospel facts or reasoning of immediate need is necessary to turn a no into a yes.

110. There are practical ways everybody can witness. Keep gospel tracts in your vehicle, pocket, or purse for ready sharing. Write a letter or send a greeting card expressing the passion of Christ for that person to be saved. Invite the unsaved to an evangelistic service. Share Christ with the person seated next to you on airplanes, buses, or trains. Talk to family members about following Christ. Ask people how you might pray for them. Get permission to leave tracts at the counter in fueling stations/restaurants frequented by truckers and tourists. Ask a minister or another experienced soulwinner to visit the lost with you. Tell your story (experience) of salvation (the why, how, and when). At motels, give a tract to the housekeeper and share a Bible promise. Bring the unsaved to church. Wear Christian attire—faith-based T-shirts, lapel pins, ties, scarves, etc. Start a Bible study on campus, at home, or at work to reach the unreached for Christ.

111. Don't shortchange soulwinning time for time spent in prayer. If an hour is needed to pray, begin praying an hour before the time to go soulwinning. At the appointed time to visit, pray briefly for the Holy Spirit's enablement and guidance and go soulwinning.

112. Make winning souls the top priority. Moody said, "God has not told me to reform the whole world. The world is like a sinking ship that cannot be kept from going down. But God has given me a lifeboat and said, 'Moody, save everyone off that ship you can.' Our chief task is to save everyone we can."

113. Make the soulwinning presentation in the home, not on the doorstep, if possible.[225] If not invited into the house, ask if you might come in for a few minutes.

114. Don't count any man hopeless. John H. Jowett said, "Where have we obtained the right to use the word 'hopeless'? What evidence or experience will justify us in saying of any man, 'He is too far gone'? Let us ransack the city. Let us rake out, if we can find him, the worst of our human race. Let us produce the sin-steeped and the lust-soddened soul, and then let us hear the word of the Master: "Believest thou that I am able to do this"? The first condition of

being capable ministers [and soulwinners] of Christ is to believe in the possibility of the world's salvation."[226]

115. The best way to start soulwinning is to begin. Charles G. Trumbull asserts, "The best way to begin in this work is to begin. The best time to begin is now. The only mistake we need really fear is the mistake of holding off."[227]

116. New converts make great soulwinners. Without instruction in soulwinning and before her baptism and church membership, the woman at Jacob's well, upon her salvation, went into the city testifying, "Come, see a man, which told me all things that ever I did: is not this the Christ?" (John 4:29). And the Bible says, "And many more believed because of His own word" (John 4:41), indicating some became believers because of her witness. New believers will benefit significantly from soulwinning training. Still, until that takes place, they should do as the Samaritan woman and immediately testify of that which Christ has done for them.

117. Permission evangelism is like the soulwinner and sinner chatting as they walk down a hallway toward a big door. Each favorable response to the soulwinner's trigger word or phrase leads them closer to the door that opens to the gospel presentation. If the sinner is unresponsive, negative, or hostile to the questions asked or trigger words used in the walk down the hallway, he's not ready to walk through the door.[228]

118. Religious conversation is relatively easy. Peter and John said, "We cannot but speak the things which we have seen and heard" (Acts 4:20). It's relatively easy to talk about Christ, who has made an eternal difference in our lives. Comfort, naturalness, and ease in soul-winning conversations may be developed in four ways.

1) Learn how to divert the secular conversation to the spiritual. 2) Follow the prompting of the Holy Spirit as to when to interject the spiritual into the conversation. 3) Realize that the unreached are generally interested in learning more about the Christian hope of forgiveness and eternal life. 4) Practice, and then practice some more.[229]

119. Create concern in the lost about their spiritual plight when they have none. R. A. Torrey said, "It is our business when a man has no concern about his salvation to go to work to produce that concern."[230] The concern is aroused by the Bible's diagnosis of man's condition before God (terminal disease of sin that separates man from God), its prognosis (eternal separation from God and saved loved ones), and its only cure (the atoning work of Christ at Calvary). Vance Havner said, "People are not brought to conviction by generalizing—we must particularize." F. B. Meyer said, "Nor is it enough to dwell in general denunciation. We must particularize till conscience cries, 'Thou art the man.'"[231] Spurgeon asserts, "A sinner will never be converted until his emotions are stirred. Unless he feels sorrow for sin, and unless he has some measure of joy in the reception of the Word, you cannot have much hope of him."[232]

120. Do not wait on a particular burden before soulwinning. The going precedes the weeping. "They that sow in tears shall reap in joy. He that goeth forth and weepeth, bearing precious seed, shall doubtless come again with rejoicing, bringing his sheaves with him" (Psalm 126:5–6). The absence of feeling "neither relieves us of our simple duty nor need hinder us in its doing."[233]

Roy Fish said, "Not our compassion for sinners, but His compassion for sinners must be our motivating factor in witnessing for Him."[234] "For the love of Christ constrains us" (2 Corinthians 5:14 WEB). J. Vernon McGee remarks, "God is saying to a great many people today, 'I want you to go and take the Word of God to those who are lost.' And they say, 'But I don't love them.' God says, 'I never asked you to love them; I asked you to go.' I cannot find anywhere that God ever asked Jonah to go because he loved the Ninevites. He said, 'Jonah, I want you to go because I love them. I love Ninevites. I want to save Ninevites. And I want you to take the message to them.'"[235]

121. Don't be shocked at what is seen in a lost man's house or by his conduct. Fish must be caught first, then cleaned.

122. Wear a smile. Let your cheerful aroma captivate the sinner's attention and interest. "The best advertisement for Christianity is a happy Christian, regardless of his lot in life."[236]

123. A significant barrier to the faith is the misconceptions arising from distorted or mistaken beliefs (multiple paths to Heaven—moral life, religious works, baptism, etc.). The skillful soulwinner clears up the misconceptions, opening the door to the gospel presentation.

124. Learn the five indicators of an excellent opportunity to witness. R. A. Torrey said, "There are five marks of a good opportunity: when one is alone, unoccupied, in good humor, communicative, and in a serious mood."[237]

125. Watch for the first signs of the Spirit's work in a soul. "Thou blessest the springing thereof" (Psalm 65:10). Spurgeon says, "I wish, dear friends, some of us had quicker eyes to see the beginning of grace in the souls of men. I am afraid some of you do not care enough about souls; consequently, you let many opportunities slip of helping the weaklings. When our hearts are set on winning souls and getting treasure for Christ, we shall soon see the first good sign and opportunity, and we shall be at once ready to do what is required."[238]

126. Keep stoking the fire to win souls. R. L. Berry said, "Close acquaintance with sin and spiritual death has worn off the sharp edge of its terribleness, and many can live at ease next door to a lost soul and never turn a hand in warning him of his awful danger."[239] The tendency is to drift away from soulwinning, never toward it. Lord, keep us from getting used to people we work with, go to school with, and socialize with dying and going to Hell.

127. The tongue of an honorable ambassador is health. "A faithful ambassador is health" (Proverbs 13:17)—not to himself, but to his Master and the people to whom he speaks the Master's Word. That which the faithful messenger says on behalf of the King (he declares all the counsel of God—Acts 20:27) brings the healing cure for the malady of sin, deliverance from the clutches of Satan, peace, and refreshment to the soul. "How beautiful upon the mountains are the feet of him that bringeth good tidings, that publisheth peace" (Isaiah 52:7). "The exclamation," asserts F. Delitzsch, "does not refer to the pretty sound of their footsteps, but their feet are as if they were winged, because it is a joyful message which they bring."[240]

In contrast, "the wicked messenger" betrays the Master's trust, dishonors the Master's name, hinders the Master's plan (Ezekiel 3:17–18), and hurts the Master's heart. Charles Bridges says, "What words can tell the awful mischief of the wicked messenger—ignorant of the worth of his commission, and utterly careless in the discharge of it! Yet the mischief returns upon his own head, laden as he is with the guilt of the blood of souls; overwhelmed himself in the eternal damnation of those who have perished through his neglect."[241]

128. Find the "clue" to the soul. Scarborough says, "There is a key that will fit every lost heart's door lock. There is a clue that will lead you to the castle door of every soul. You can take the fortress if you can find the key, the clue....Prayer, spiritual insight, the guiding Holy Spirit will show it to you. If you are in touch with the mind of God, who knows all things, you can walk in a certain path and find the way to the citadel of souls."[242]

129. Never distort or twist the Scriptures to gain a soul. Jesus didn't; we mustn't (Mark 10:22; John 6:60–66). Stay above board with the means employed. Jesus never tried to win a soul by ruse (Romans 12:17).

130. Rebuff the pressure to be silent. The Sanhedrin tried to silence the disciples from speaking about Jesus with threats of being charged with a heinous crime. But it was met with the bold, defiant declaration of Peter and John, "Whether it be right in the sight of God to hearken unto you more than unto God, judge ye. For we cannot but speak the things which we have seen and heard" (Acts 4:19–20). Matthew Henry said, "There is not a greater service done to the Devil's kingdom than the silencing of faithful ministers [soulwinners] and putting those under a bushel that are the lights of the world."[243] Brazenly speak up for Christ when told to shut up.

> Must I be carried to the skies
>     On flowery beds of ease,
> While others fought to win the prize
>     And sailed through bloody seas?
>
> ~Isaac Watts (1724)

131. Most unbelievers would welcome the presentation of the Gospel. Barna Group asked unbelievers, "Would you be willing to listen to a gospel presentation from someone passionate about his faith?" Seventy percent responded, "Yes."

132. The least gifted, the believer of one talent, ought to engage in soulwinning as faithfully as the most gifted, the servant with many talents.[244]

133. Idleness in soulwinning provides Satan the opportunity to lead sinners deeper into the quagmire of sin in one form or another, bolster their resistance to the Gospel, sow seeds of doubt or confusion in their minds about the Gospel, and prevent their rescue to a better life presently and Heaven hereafter.

134. Conversion is God's work. Of Lydia it is recorded: "The Lord opened her heart to give heed unto the things which were spoken by Paul" (Acts 16:14 KJ21). When Lydia heard the Word that Paul spoke, the Lord opened her heart to receive it. The soulwinner plants and cultivates, but God causes the seed to germinate and grow. Paul said, "I planted the seed in your hearts, and Apollos watered it, but it was God who made it grow. It's not important who does the planting, or who does the watering. What's important is that God makes the seed grow" (1 Corinthians 3:6–7 NLT).

Salvation is not based on evangelistic plans, booklets, gospel presentations, or ability. It's God's work from start to finish. "Not by might, nor by power, but by My Spirit, saith the Lord of hosts" (Zechariah 4:6). Utilize plans and booklets, a clear gospel presentation, and trained ability to reach the lost, the entire while depending upon the power of the Holy Spirit to quicken the life to salvation.

135. Entertain one conversation at a time. The silent partner in the visit must refrain from being drawn into a second conversation, which would distract from the primary one.

136. Schedule soulwinning days and times. Epictetus said, "Events do not just happen, but arrive by appointment." Pablo Picasso stated, "Our goals can only be reached through a vehicle of a plan, in

which we must fervently believe, and upon which we must vigorously act. There is no other route to success."

137. Set a witnessing goal. Make a goal like D. L. Moody to witness to one person a day. Make a goal to witness to at least one person a week or five people a month. Make a goal to participate in your church's weekly visitation night.

138. In presenting the Gospel, stay in one Bible book for calm and ease. Trying to flip to various texts in different books can be unnerving in the heat of an encounter, especially to the soulwinning beginner.

139. Strike while the iron is hot. R. G. Lee warns, "Doors once opened but unentered may close again. Minds made susceptible but not won for Christ may turn away and become hardened. Truth resisted once is easier to resist next time."[245]

140. Seek to convert those who have been overlooked and avoided. "Let it be the effort of Christian people," saith Spurgeon, "to go after those that nobody else is going after; the best fruit will be gleaned from boughs hitherto untouched."[246] Be a Ruth and glean the fields for the souls either unwanted or unreached by others (Ruth 2:3).

141. Chew gum inconspicuously. Chewing gum is to be a deterrent to bad breath, not to the witness.

142. Show consideration for the health and well-being of others. Keep your nasal congestion, sneezing, and fever at home. Nobody wants strangers in their home who are sick, masked or not.

143. Departing from home without a New Testament and tracts in the pocket heightens the likelihood a witness won't happen for Christ that day.

144. The magnet that draws the lost to the Christian faith is the *truth* about God's love, Christ's deity, atonement, resurrection, and the eternal significance of each. Lord Halifax said, "Men will not be brought to embrace the Christian religion because it is recommended as expedient, or necessary, or full of moral values. But they will go on their knees if they can come to feel that it is true." George Sweazey states, "Evangelism will find an audience when it makes plain that it is offering solid facts about God and man and the

universe."[247] The lost are asking with Pilate, "What is truth?" Convincingly and soundly, be prepared to answer.

145. Think upon the state of a lost soul. Saith Spurgeon, "If you would be useful, dear brothers and sisters...you must think much upon the divine realities until they move and stir your souls; that men are dying and perishing, that Hell is filling, that Christ is dishonored, that souls are not converted to Christ, that the Holy Ghost is grieved, that the kingdom does not come to God, but that Satan rules and reigns—all this ought to be well considered by us."[248]

146. Soulwinning is hard work. "As things are," said William Nowell, "soulwinning is just about the toughest task to which man can put his hand." That was said over a hundred years ago and hasn't changed. Samuel Chadwick stated, "Soulwinning is acknowledged to be exacting as it is glorious. It is a work that makes demands upon the brain and heart and soul. No work requires such tactful wisdom, diligent labor, and earnest prayer." Billy Sunday stated, "Winning souls is a difficult form of work. It is more difficult than preaching; it is more difficult than attending conventions or giving goods to the poor. You can pin on a badge, usher people to their seats, pass the collection plate, be an elder or deacon or a steward; you can go to church, sing in the choir, be a member of a home or foreign missionary society—the Devil will even let you attend Bible conferences—but the minute you begin to do personal work to try to get somebody to take a stand for Christ, all the devils in Hell will be on your back, for they know that is a challenge to the Devil and to his forces. The work of leading people to Christ by personal effort [is]...hard."[249]

147. Keep the same witnessing partner for effectiveness until it is prudent to change. Note that a change in companions may be needed to mentor another in the work, learn new approaches and methods, or become *more* effective.

148. Take three deep, slow breaths to help ease jitters before a visit.

149. Soulwinning is most effective on a personal basis. Preach and teach to win souls, but realize the most successful way to bring the lost to Christ is one-to-one. John R. Rice said, "The winning of individuals by individuals in personal conversation is the main way

to win souls."[250] Eighty-three percent of new believers are led to Christ through personal soulwinning.

150. The greatest thing that can be done is for one to leave his or her spiritual thumb mark on a soul. Andrew Bonar said, "There will not be a redeemed soul in Heaven that does not have a human thumb mark upon it." So live and witness that many in Heaven will bear your thumb mark.

151. Never quit on a soul. Many in Heaven were thought by some to be unreachable. But they were wrong. J. C. Ryle challenges: "Let us learn never to despair of the salvation of anyone, as long as he lives. The arm of grace is very long and can reach those who seem very far off. The Holy Spirit can change any heart. The blood of Christ can cleanse away any sin. Let us pray on and hope on for others, however unlikely their salvation may appear to be at present. We shall see many in Heaven whom we never expected to see there."[251]

152. The arm of flesh will fail you. The power of the Spirit flows through the soulwinner like electricity through a wire, accomplishing the needed task (as long as He is allowed to work in the life).[252] Apart from that power, despite expertise and logic, soulwinning is futile. "God hath spoken once; twice have I heard this; that power belongeth unto God" (Psalm 62:11).

153. When you are using a gospel tract or booklet, prevent the prospect from reading ahead. Maintain complete focus on what is shared in the booklet by holding it open solely to the page being presented.

154. The trajectory of the witness is determined within the first two to three minutes of an encounter based on the person's interest, receptivity, biblical knowledge, time available, and disclosure or discernment of belief.

155. Always magnify Christ. "He must increase, but I must decrease" (John 3:30). Saith Spurgeon, "Say much of what the Savior has done for you, but say little of what you have done for the Lord. Do not utter a self-glorifying sentence."[253]

156. Home visitation is ideal but increasingly impeded. When presenting a witness in the home is impossible, invite the person out for coffee, to your office, or an outing conducive to the objective.

157. Be a sweet-smelling fragrance of Christ. "In fact, God thinks of us as a perfume that brings Christ to everyone" (2 Corinthians 2:15 CEV). Only to the measure that we diffuse the fragrance of Christ by conduct, concern, disposition, and message (His Word and works) will the lost be attracted to Him. It is the magnetism of Christ and by the Holy Spirit's power, our magnification of Christ, that without distinction, men are drawn to salvation (John 12:32; Jeremiah 31:3).

158. Biographies of great soulwinners (Whitefield, Moody, Wesley, John Hyde, Spurgeon) will inflame the heart to go soulwinning and guide how.

159. Launch out into the deep. Spurgeon asserts, "We would do better if we went further afield. We are fools to waste time in the shallows of our churches while the deep teems with waiting fish. Invite the often invited, certainly, but do not forget those who have never been invited as yet have not been hardened by refusals."[254]

160. Pray and don't lose heart. "Men ought always to pray, and not to faint" (Luke 18:1). Hallesby writes, "When you begin to grow tired of the quiet, unnoticed work of praying, then remember that He who seeth in secret shall reward you openly. He has heard your prayers and knows exactly what you have accomplished by means of them for the salvation of souls. If not before, then on the Great Day, you will come bringing in the sheaves, the fruit of your labors."[255]

161. Questions are a means to get people talking. Questions about family and work often open into questions about spiritual things.

In his autobiography, Spurgeon details how he used questions to share the Gospel with a waterman on a boat. "Whilst sitting in the boat, wishing to talk to him about religious matters, I began the conversation by asking him about his family. He told me that the cholera had visited his home and that he had lost no less than thirteen of his relatives, one after another, by death. My question and the man's answer prepared the way for a dialogue" that he said continued with the question, "Have you, my friend, a good hope of Heaven if you should die?"

If the witness was the means to open the man's eyes to the need for salvation and bring him to Christ, Spurgeon did not know. But he said, "I had the satisfaction of knowing that I had at least set before him God's way of salvation in language he could easily understand."

162. Find encouragement in the fact that the godliest and most gifted of saints often find personal work challenging. Not even Spurgeon, the renowned London pastor, found soulwinning easy. Despite pulpit and newspaper soulwinning to the masses and instructive lectures about it to his Pastor's College students, Spurgeon found the task done on a personal basis a struggle. In his autobiography, he states, "I often envy those of my brethren who can go up to individuals and talk to them with freedom about their souls. I do not always find myself able to do so, though, when I have been Divinely aided in such service, I have had a large reward."[256]

163. Don't let the criticism of the way you do soulwinning impede it. A lady criticized Moody's method of winning people to the Lord, to which he responded, "I agree with you. I don't like the way I do it either. Tell me, how do you do it?"

The lady replied, "I don't do it."

Moody countered, "I like my way of doing it better than your way of not doing it."

164. Plow new ground; fish in new ponds. "Continuing to plow upon the same old soil again and again, we can hardly expect to reap much of a harvest. Hearts have become seared, and consciences have become callous."[257]

165. Never count yourself too "big" to stoop to witness. Moody says, "When a man gets so high that he can't reach down and save poor sinners, there is something wrong."

166. The four letters of FORM provide guidance to the witness. *F*—talk about *family*. *O*—talk about *occupation*. *R*—talk about *religious* background/church affiliation. *M*—share the *message* of salvation.

167. Appointments avoid waste of time.

168. The more the Good News is exclusively shared, the greater the success in soulwinning. Spurgeon asserts, "He will succeed best who keeps closest to soul-saving truth. Now, all truth is not soul-saving. He that keeps to the simple story of the cross, tells men over and over again that whosoever believeth in Christ is not condemned, that to be saved nothing is wanted but a simple trust in the crucified Redeemer; he whose ministry is much made up of the glorious story of the cross, the sufferings of the dying Lamb, the mercy of God; he who cries, in fact, from day to day, 'Behold the Lamb of God, which taketh away the sin of the world,' he is likely to be a soul-winner, especially if he adds to this much prayer for souls, much anxious desire that men may be brought to Jesus."[258]

169. When none are ever won, the fault perhaps lies in the believer's spiritual state, readiness or preparedness, theology, or methodology (Psalm 126:6; Psalm 139:23–24).

170. Mental and spiritual readiness is essential. Says Spurgeon, "It is no child's play, nor a thing to be achieved while we are half asleep, nor to be attempted without deep consideration, nor to be carried on without gracious help from the only-wise God, our Savior."[259]

171. The best, not necessarily the easiest, place to start soulwinning is with family, friends, business associates, and classmates.

172. An uplifting commendation at the start often lends to gospel receptivity later (Proverbs 18:24).

173. "Do not pass out pleasing platitudes to a careless procrastinator."[260] The Bible says, "He, that being often reproved hardeneth his neck, shall suddenly be destroyed, and that without remedy" (Proverbs 29:1).

174. If possible, close all visits, objective attained or not, with prayer.

175. Confer with experienced soulwinners in difficult encounters.

# 15

# The Soulwinners' Reward

"Now he that planteth and he that watereth are one: and every man *shall receive his own reward according to his own labor*" (1 Corinthians 3:8). Exclusive rewards, which serve as honorable motivators for soulwinning, are reserved for people who win souls.

1. The reward of personal delight in seeing a soul gloriously converted. The psalmist testified, "They that sow in tears shall reap in joy" (Psalm 126:5). Saith Spurgeon, "If you are eager for real joy, I am persuaded that no joy of growing wealthy, no joy of influence over your fellow creatures, no joy of any other sort, can ever compare with the rapture of saving a soul from death[261]....never did I know perfect, overflowing, unutterable happiness of the purest and most ennobling order, till I first heard of one who had sought and found a Savior through my means."[262] "Beyond all controversy," he said, "it is a joy worth worlds to win souls."[263]

Saith Scarborough, "Go after souls. There is no joy like it." Moody attests, "There is no greater honor than to be the instrument in God's hands of leading one person out of the kingdom of Satan into the glorious light of Heaven." Paul testified that the souls he won would be his joy and crown of rejoicing (1 Thessalonians 2:19).

Four worlds are made happy when a soul is won. Happiness floods the convert's life and that of his family and friends, the saints in Heaven, and him that won the person. Watchman Nee said, "Beloved, there are two big days in the life of a believer: the day on which he believes in the Lord and every day after that when he leads someone to faith in Christ."[264]

Saith Leonard Sanderson, "When one sees another soul come to the Savior, all the bells of his heart begin ringing in a melody similar to that of the day of his own salvation. When he feels the warm handclasp of the one who has just said, 'I do,' it is like an electric current that connects with Heaven for a time. Joy inexpressible in human language is experienced."[265]

2. The reward of making a difference in another's life. James says, "Let him know, that he which converteth the sinner from the error of his way shall save a soul from death, and shall hide a multitude of sins" (James 5:20). Spurgeon said, "If we had to preach to thousands year after year, and never rescued but one soul, that one soul would be a full reward for all our labor, for a soul is of countless price."

3. The reward of knowing that to win a soul is the most outstanding work and achievement in life. No greater work has been assigned to the church than to rescue souls "by snatching them from the fire" (Jude 23 CSB).

4. The reward of bringing pleasure to God. "The richest reward," saith Spurgeon, "lies in pleasing God and causing the Redeemer to see the results of the travail of His soul!"[266] Spurgeon continues, saying, "Let me ask you a question. What would you give to cause a thrill of pleasure in the heart of the beloved Redeemer? Remember the grief you cost Him and the pangs which shot through Him on your account so that He might deliver you from your sin and its consequences. Don't you long to make Him glad? When you bring others to His feet, you give Him joy."[267]

5. The reward of sharing in the fruit of the ones won. He that wins another is credited alongside him with the souls he wins. Kimball, the shoe clerk who won Moody, though never leaving Chicago, was credited with Moody for the million souls he brought to Christ worldwide. To our knowledge, Andrew never preached a sermon. Still, by bringing Peter to Jesus, he became, as Robert Sumner says, the spiritual grandfather of the three thousand souls Peter won at Pentecost (John 1:41–42).

6. The reward of seeing those won on earth in Heaven. Paul says, "For what is it we live for, that gives us hope and joy and is our proud reward and crown? It is you! Yes, you will bring us much joy as we stand together before our Lord Jesus Christ when he comes back again" (1 Thessalonians 2:19 TLB). He anticipated seeing his trophies of grace (converts to Christ) in Heaven and declared that would be a great delight and joy.

If a soul is in Heaven by my efforts, I shall feel like Samuel Rutherford, who said, "My Heaven will be two Heavens in

Immanuel's Land." How many people are now alive forever, and will we meet again in Heaven because we shared Jesus with them? (On the other hand, how many will be absent because we failed to speak to them about Him?)

Matthew Henry says, "Those that turn men to righteousness, turn sinners from the errors of their ways, and help to save their souls from death (James 5:20) will share in the glory of those they have helped to Heaven, which will be a great addition to their own glory."[268]

Perhaps in Heaven, someday, to me
    Some sainted one shall come and say,
"All hail, beloved, but for thee
    My soul to death had fallen a prey."
And, oh, the rapture of the thought,
One soul to glory to have brought!

                    ~Author unknown.

7. The reward of receiving the Crown of Rejoicing at God's throne. "You are our hope, our joy, and the crown we will take pride in when our Lord Jesus Christ comes" (1 Thessalonians 2:19 NCV). Theologians often refer to this crown as the crown of soulwinning. Saints who win souls to Christ will be the recipients of this crown.

8. The reward of shining as the stars forever. "They that turn many to righteousness [shall shine] as the stars for ever and ever" (Daniel 12:3). As the stars in the firmament shine brilliantly, some more so than others, just so the saints that win souls will shine out God's glory forever as their reward.

# 16

# The Soulwinners' Model

No passage in the Bible is more helpful to the soulwinners' approach to the lost than Jesus' encounter with the woman at Jacob's well in John 4. From the beginning to the end, John details how Jesus won the woman to saving faith (John 4:6–25).

*Step One*. Jesus saw her as a sinner in need of salvation. The woman's water jug was full, but her heart was empty. See people as He saw her—empty souls thirsting for hope, healing, and happiness. Spurgeon says, "Our Lord's object was to bring the woman to seek salvation of Him."[269]

*Step Two*. He refused to allow her sinful lifestyle or the racial prejudice that existed between the Jews and the Samaritans to hinder the witness. Many would have said she was an unlikely prospect—but not Jesus. Don't allow people's race or lifestyle to impede your presentation of the Gospel to them. Soulwinning crosses every barrier to bring man to God.

*Step Three*. Jesus engages the woman by requesting water to drink. Requests and questions help initiate the gospel witness.

*Step Four*. Jesus connects the woman's need for salvation with the well from which she was drawing water. The physical was used to preach the spiritual. Jesus often used parables to clarify and teach theological truth. Paul also used physical pegs on which to hang spiritual truths. He used the peg of a boxer in the ring (1 Corinthians 9:26), a runner in a race (1 Corinthians 9:24), a farmer in the field (2 Timothy 2:6), and a soldier in battle (2 Timothy 2:3) to convey the gospel message.

*Step Five*. He kept the witness simple. Jesus knew all the theological lingo but shelved it to share the Gospel in a way the woman could comprehend. All men are like little children in their understanding of the gospel message. Keep the cookies on the bottom shelf.

*Step Six*. Jesus skillfully unmasked her sin and confronted it. Tactfully, the soulwinner must point out sin, its consequences, and its only remedy (Romans 3:23 and Romans 6:23).

*Step Seven*. He was prepared to handle her opposing theological views and objections. Believers ought to be ready to thwart religious misconceptions and flawed theology as much as possible when such things impede the witness (1 Peter 3:15). Ignorance and deception often keep man from knowing "the unspeakable gift" of salvation ("living water") in Christ Jesus. Expose and erase these things, and the door opens to eternal life.

*Step Eight.* Jesus refused to be sidetracked by the woman's questions. He turned her questions into a springboard to drive the gospel message home to her heart. In witnessing, always "wrestle" the conversation from issues they may raise back to the person's need. Stay on task.

*Step Nine.* Jesus listened to the woman. Soulwinners are good listeners. Listening provides insight into the person's misconceptions about salvation (as it did for Jesus about this woman), spiritual knowledge, and difficulties with becoming a Christian.

*Step Ten.* Jesus did not compromise the message of salvation. Stay true to the message and means of saving grace through repentance of sin and faith in Christ. The hard fact is that some, in hearing the Gospel, will walk away, as did the rich young ruler, counting its cost too great. Jesus said, "If any man will come after me, let him deny himself, and take up his cross daily, and follow me" (Luke 9:23).

*Step Eleven.* Jesus cited how the means of salvation could be received. "Thou wouldest have asked." It must be requested in prayer by faith. Through prayer, man accesses Christ to forgive sin and save him (the sinner's prayer). Note, the principle for the sinner's prayer is in the Bible, though the title "sinner's prayer" is not (Romans 10:9–13; Acts 2:21).

There are many words that are not found in the Bible but whose concept is, such as *Trinity* (Genesis 1:26; Isaiah 48:16; Matthew 28:19), *atheism* (Psalm 14:1), *sovereignty* (1 Chronicles 29:11–12; Psalm 103:19), *incarnation* (John 1:14), *monotheism* (Deuteronomy 6:4; 2 Samuel 7:22; 1 Timothy 2:5), *rapture* (1 Thessalonians 4:16–17), etc.

The calling on the name of the Lord ("sinner's prayer") is baseless and thus futile if not preceded by the presentation of the Gospel (the fact and meaning of man's sin and the truth of the death and resurrection of Jesus) and precipitated by an understanding of that message with godly sorrow over one's sin toward God with the desire to change.

*Step Twelve.* Jesus' best effort was given to win the woman. Soulwinning is absorbing, wholehearted work (John 4:34).[270] He didn't hold back, but spoke to her as if she were the only lost soul on earth. Make each witness count. It may be the person's last chance of salvation; don't shortchange the effort.

Charles Trumbull said, "No opportunity is so slight or trifling that it can be safely passed by." John B. Gough said of the one word of Christ another shared with him that won him, "It may be a small matter to you to speak the one word for Christ that wins a needy soul—a small matter to you, but it is everything to him."[271]

*Step Thirteen.* Jesus drew the net. When the woman responded to the gospel presentation, she was gloriously saved at the first asking. E. Y. Mullins said, "Jesus always respected human personality. He never sought to coerce the will. He never sought to overwhelm it by appeals or to influence it by any undue motives. He sought to recognize under all circumstances man's freedom and personal responsibility."[272]

End a witness with an invitation to be saved (apart from coercion) "then and there." Ask, "Is there any good reason why you cannot call upon the Lord to be your Lord and Savior right now?" or "Will you pray with me to receive Christ into your life as Lord and Savior?"

Note, evidence of the woman's conversion is manifest in the bold witness she made to the people of the city (John 4:29) that caused many to believe (John 4:39). Roland Leavell states, "When a man meets Christ, he learns to love souls."[273] This woman did—as do all others.

# 17

# The Soulwinners' Apologetics

Apologetics is a verbal defense (evidence and reason) of Christian belief. Knowing what is believed and why it is believed enhances the believer's certainty and confidence in that belief (edification) while enabling a ready defense of it to all that ask (evangelization). "Always be ready to answer everyone who asks you to explain about the hope you have" (1 Peter 3:15 NCV). Norman Geisler states, "God has used evidence and reason in some way to reach virtually all adults who come to Christ."[274]

### The Belief in the Existence of God

"But there is a God in heaven" (Daniel 2:28). What arguments are there for believing in the existence of God?

*The cosmological argument.* For every effect, there has to be a cause. There has to be an explanation for all that exists; nothing just exists. It follows that if there is a cause for all that exists, there must be a "first cause" to set things in motion. There has to be a beginning "Domino." This "first cause" is God. He is the originating "domino" (Creator) that has set the world in motion.

*The teleological argument.* Where there is "design," there must be a "designer." The possibility of a watch's intrinsic parts just coming together for its formation and accurate function is so far out that it is absurd to consider. The same applies to the intrinsic design and operation of the universe. Where there is a watch, there is a watchmaker, and behind the incredible, complex universe is a Master Designer who is God. W. H. Fitchett said, "The absolute proof of God's existence is thus found in the relations in which the mindless elements of the universe are set with each other, producing an order of which they are not only incapable but unconscious."[275]

*The anthropological argument.* The fact of man and the recognition of moral law points to a Creator and Lawgiver. That is God. The Bible says, "For when Gentiles who do not have the Law do instinctively the things of the Law, these, not having the Law, are a law to themselves, in that they show the work of the Law written in their hearts, their conscience bearing witness and their thoughts alternately accusing or else defending them" (Romans 2:14–15 NASB).

Lewis Chafer states, "There are...moral features in man's constitution which may be traced back to find their origin in God....A blind force...could never produce a man with intellect, sensibility, will, conscience, and inherent belief in a Creator."[276] W. A. Criswell states, "The fact that we are persons leads one to conclude that wherever we came from, whoever did it, must Himself have been a person of mind and intelligence. That is God."[277]

The constitution for the fact of God is divinely stamped in man's mind. The worship of a Supreme Being throughout the world gives credence to God, who created man with that inward thirst and hunger to know and worship Him. Augustine said, "Thou hast made us for thyself, O Lord, and our heart is restless until it finds its rest in thee."

*The theological argument.* "In the beginning was the Word, and the Word was with God, and the Word was God" (John 1:1). Biblical writers did not endeavor to prove the existence of God. To them, that was self-evident. However, the Bible's remarkable unity, historical accuracy, archeological finds, and millions of testimonies regarding its trustworthiness prove the existence of its Author, God. Within its inspired sacred pages, God discloses Himself.

*The Resurrection Argument.* The Resurrection of Jesus is a miracle that only the Supreme Maker and Controller of the cosmos could bring about. That is God.

Billy Graham said, "There is more evidence that Jesus rose from the dead than there is that Julius Caesar ever lived or that Alexander the Great died at the age of thirty-three." "There exists such overwhelming evidence...that no intelligent jury in the world could fail to bring a verdict that the resurrection story is true." (Lord Darling, former Chief Justice of England)

*The testimonial argument.* "One thing I know, that, whereas I was blind, now I see" (John 9:25). Grave proof of the fact of God is found in the miraculous change (intelligently, morally, and spiritually) that happens to the person who embraces Him by faith.

No explanation exists for the transformation outside the supernatural intervention of God. "A new heart also will I give you, and a new spirit will I put within you: and I will take away the stony heart out of your flesh, and I will give you an heart of flesh" (Ezekiel 36:26). "What a wonderful change in my heart has been wrought since Jesus came into my heart."

Man's denial of God's existence doth not in one iota alter the fact. Spurgeon says, "If the sinner could by his atheism destroy the God whom he hates, there was some sense, although much wickedness, in his infidelity; but as denying the existence of fire does not prevent its burning a man who is in it, so doubting the existence of God will not stop the Judge of all the earth from destroying the rebel who breaks His laws. Nay, this atheism is a crime which much provokes Heaven and will bring down terrible vengeance on the fool who indulges it." Augustine validly says, "He who denies the existence of God has some reason for wishing that God did not exist."

Wernher von Braun said, "My experiences with science led me to God. They challenge science to prove the existence of God. *But must we really light a candle to see the sun?*" Nobody is blinder than the person who refuses to see. The Scriptures say, "The fool hath said in his heart, there is no God" (Psalm 14:1; Psalm 53:1).

### The Belief That the Bible Is the Word of God

"It is in truth, the word of God" (1 Thessalonians 2:13). What is the basis for believing that the Bible is the Word of God? While the Bible validates itself through an array of internal supports of its reliability—consistency, multiple witnesses, verifiable history—it is also validated by many external pieces of evidence.

*The archeological reason.* The Bible is confirmed to be authentic by over one hundred archeological discoveries. Scholars once denied the existence and description of the Hittite nation as factual until the Hittite capital and records were discovered at Bogazkoy, Turkey.[278] Skeptics thought Solomon's wealth was greatly exaggerated until recent discoveries revealed that wealth in antiquity was concentrated with the king.[279] Some claimed that there was never an Assyrian king named Sargon (Isaiah 20:1) until his palace was discovered in Khorsabad, Iraq.[280] King Belshazzar (Daniel 5) was also considered fictitious until tablets were found showing that he was Nabonidus' son who served as coregent in Babylon.[281]

Outside the Bible, no documentation was known to give credence to the existence of Pontius Pilate. But in 1961, archeologists discovered a stone inscription at Caesarea that bore Pontius Pilate's inscription honoring the Roman emperor Tiberius. Coins dating from Pilate's gubernatorial rule have also been found.[282]

The discovery of the Dead Sea Scrolls (February 20, 1947), the greatest in the twentieth century, substantiates the integrity and accuracy of Scripture. The archeologist's blade is ever confirming the Bible as truth and will continue to do so until the return of Christ.

*The scientific reason.* Francis Bacon says, "A little science estranges a man from God; a lot of science brings him back."[283] The Bible contains scientific facts unknown to man for hundreds of years (about the stars, moon, oceans, planets, the chemistry of blood, etc.). How could that be? An all-knowing God divinely authored it. These scientific facts give credence to the authority of the Bible.

*The prophetic reason.* "Fulfilled prophecy," states John MacArthur, "is perhaps the greatest proof that the Word of God is true. It carries the weight of proof for the Word of God further than any other single element of Scripture."[284]

Micah prophesied the place where Jesus would be born, in Bethlehem Ephrathah (Micah 5:2), and He *was* born there—700 years later. Isaiah prophesied that Jesus would be born of a virgin (Isaiah 7:14), and He was.

Daniel prophesied the exact year that Jesus would die (Daniel 9:24–27), and He died precisely then. Isaiah prophesied hundreds of years before Jesus' birth that He would be buried with the rich (Isaiah 53:9). This was fulfilled despite Jesus' being poor. He was buried in the unused tomb of a wealthy man, something unheard of before this. The same prophecy declared that Jesus would die with the wicked, which happened when He was crucified between two thieves.

Jeremiah prophesied that the Messiah would descend from King David (Jeremiah 23:5–6). Jesus was, according to Matthew 1. Isaiah foretold the rejection of Christ by His unbelieving people (Isaiah 53). This prophecy was fulfilled (John 1:11).

*The experiential reason.* To the archeological, scientific, and prophetic objective evidence for the Bible's being the Word of God, add the subjective evidence of personal experience. I know the Bible is the divine Word of God due to the Holy Spirit's illumination and confirmation to me that it is and because it does what it says it will do for me, in me, and through me. I can point to promises and precepts in the Bible that have been fulfilled in my life regarding salvation, forgiveness, strength, comfort, service, and more, as can millions of other believers.

A little boy had a tummy ache, and his mother asked why. He said, "I've been eating green apples."

The mother inquired, "How do you know the green apples are causing the stomachache?"

"Because," the boy replied, "I have inside information." How do I know the Bible is the Word of God? I have inside information. Every born-again believer does.

"The Holy Spirit," declares R. A. Torrey, "sets His seal in the soul of every believer to the divine authority of the Bible. Christ says, 'My sheep hear my voice.' God's children know His voice, and I know that the voice which speaks to me from the pages of that Book is the voice of my Father. Everyone can have that testimony. John 7:17 tells you how to get it: 'If any man will do his will, he shall know of the doctrine, whether it be of God.'" Of the Bible, B. B. Warfield said, "How unquestionably we must receive its statements of fact, bow before its enunciations of duty, tremble before its warnings, and rest upon its promises."[285]

The bottom line? Charlie H. Campbell says, "We're not asking people to believe what the Bible says about God, just 'because it says so.' No. We want people to believe the Bible because of the wealth of good evidence that has demonstrated the Bible to be trust-worthy...hundreds of fulfilled prophecies... thousands of archaeological discoveries...numerous details in the Bible that have been corroborated by extrabiblical historical sources, and so on." D. James

Kennedy said, "Never has a skeptic been able to overturn or overthrow the evidences for the inspiration of the Scriptures."[286]

### The Belief that Jesus is the Son of God

"God was manifest in the flesh, justified in the Spirit, seen of angels, preached unto the Gentiles, believed on in the world, received up into glory" (1 Timothy 3:16). The truth of Christianity hinges on the deity of Christ, which is not without confirmation.

*His deity is confirmed by God at His baptism.* As He was being baptized in the river Jordan, "a voice from heaven, [was heard] saying, This is my beloved Son, in whom I am well pleased" (Matthew 3:17). A. W. Pink says, "Certainty that Christ is 'the Son of the living God' comes not by listening to the labored arguments of seminary professors, nor by studying books on Christian evidences, but by believing what God has said about His Son in the Holy Scriptures."[287]

*His deity is confirmed by equality with the Father.* In John, Jesus is shown to be equal with the Father in works, wisdom, judgment, raising the dead, authority, honor, and power (John 5:17–27). A comparison of Colossians 1:16 with Genesis 1:1 shows Him to be equal to the Father in creation. T. F. Torrance says, "Christ is not just a sort of *locum tenens* or a kind of 'double' for God in His absence, but the incarnate presence of Yahweh."[288] R. C. Sproul said, "What we celebrate at Christmas is not so much the birth of a baby, but the incarnation of God Himself."

*His deity is confirmed by the virgin birth.* Isaiah prophesized 700 years before the birth of Jesus that Messiah would be conceived of a virgin (Isaiah 7:14). Christ's immaculate conception and the manger at Bethlehem reveal that He is the promised Messiah, the Son of God who came to earth on a redemptive mission.

*His deity is confirmed by the sinlessness of life.* "He committed no sin, neither was deceit found in his mouth" (1 Peter 2:22 ESV). Pilate could find "no fault in Him," nor can any man. Why? He is the Son of God. Strauss said, "Jesus had a conscience unclouded by the memory of sin."

*His deity is confirmed by Himself.* Christ asserted that He existed before Abraham and was the Jehovah of the Old Testament (John 8:56–59). He declared Himself to be the only Way or Door to Heaven (John 14:6; 10:9) and that "my kingdom is not of this world" (John 18:36). He asserted, "I and my Father are one" (John 10:30). And the clincher to His confirmation of His deity was the promise that when He was crucified and His body was buried, "in three days I will raise it up" (John 2:19)—which happened.

*His deity is confirmed by His miracles.* The miracles of Christ are documented in Scripture and external sources, such as the *Acts of Pontius Pilate*, the testimony of the Jewish historian Josephus, and the Sanhedrin, Jesus' enemies. R. C. Sproul wrote, "They [genuine miracles], and they alone, ultimately prove that Christ is the Son of God and that the Bible is the Word of God. All other 'evidence' is corroborative."[289]

*His deity is confirmed by the prophecies regarding the Messiah.* Norman Geisler states, "All the evidence points to Jesus as the divinely appointed fulfillment of the Messianic prophecies. He was God's Man, confirmed by God's signs."[290] Said Fritz Ridenour, "The Old Testament contains over 300 references to the Messiah that were fulfilled in Jesus Christ. Computations using the science of probability on just 8 of these prophecies show the chance that someone could have fulfilled all eight prophecies is 1 in $10^{17}$, or 1 in 100 quadrillion."

*His deity is confirmed by the disciples.* Of Christ, Paul says, "Who is the image of the invisible God, the firstborn of every creature: For by him were all things created, that are in heaven, and that are in earth, visible and invisible, whether they be thrones, or dominions, or principalities, or powers: all things were created by him, and for him: And he is before all things, and by him all things consist" (Colossians 1:15–17). Spurgeon asserts, "How can anyone read this passage and yet say Jesus is only a man? By what twisting of words can such language as this be applied to the most eminent prophet or apostle who ever lived? Surely, He must be God by whom all things were created, and by whom all things consist."

To the question of Jesus to Peter, "Whom say ye that I am?" came the immediate reply, "Thou art the Christ, the Son of the living God" (Matthew 16:16). And later, Peter acted as the spokesman of all the disciples and said, "Lord, to whom shall we go? thou hast the words of eternal life. And *we* believe and *are sure* that thou art that Christ, the Son of the living God" (John 6:68–69).

*His deity is confirmed by His substitutionary death.* Saith Criswell, "The death of Christ makes provision for the propitiation [cancellation of sin's effect] for the sins of the whole world. Men may reject the Lord's substitutionary death, accepting condemnation instead, but Jesus died for all. The word may be translated as 'satisfaction' in the sense that Christ's death satisfied the just demands of God's holy judgment of sin."[291]

*His deity is confirmed by the resurrection.* "And declared to be the Son of God with power, according to the spirit of holiness, by the resurrection from the dead" (Romans 1:4). Proof of Christ's deity is manifest in His being the first to rise from the dead (1 Corinthians 15:20), for which there is a preponderance of evidence.

*His deity is confirmed by the Scriptures.* The Bible says, "For in him [Christ] the whole fullness of deity dwells bodily, and you have been filled in him, who is the head of all rule and authority" (Colossians 2:9–10 ESV). See Hebrews 1:2–3. Saith Oswald Sanders, "The deity of Christ is the key doctrine of the Scriptures. Reject it, and the Bible becomes a jumble of words without any unifying theme. Accept it, and the Bible becomes an intelligible and ordered revelation of God in the person of Jesus Christ."

*His deity is confirmed by the sinner's transformation.* "Therefore if any man be in Christ, he is a new creature: old things are passed away; behold, all things are become new" (2 Corinthians 5:17). E. Y. Mullins states, "The morally transformed man proves the deity of Christ, proves His presence in religious experience, first of all, because no man has moral resources to transform himself. It proves the deity of Christ because when the sinner turns to Christ, he gets the response. Christ invites him, and he responds. He calls, and Christ answers. In his outward life, a new force begins to work, a new design, a new labor working to an end. But especially within is there Another, one with whom there is fellowship, to whom he becomes passionately devoted, whose presence is happiness and whose absence is sorrow."[292]

*His deity will be confirmed by His return.* The final verification of Christ's deity will be given at His second coming (John 14:1–3). At that moment, all men will acknowledge that Jesus is the Son of God and Savior of the world and say with the Centurion, "Truly this was the Son of God" (Matthew 27:54).

### The Belief in the Resurrection of Christ

"Blessed be the God and Father of our Lord Jesus Christ, which according to his abundant mercy hath begotten us again unto a lively hope by the resurrection of Jesus Christ from the dead" (1 Peter 1:3).

*There is reason to believe in the resurrection of Christ because of what happened before it.*

First, concerning prophecy, the fact that prophecies foretold Christ's death and resurrection hundreds of years in advance proves it. More than 950 years before it happened (Psalm 22:7–18), it was prophesied that Messiah upon the Cross would be railed upon (passersby, Matthew 27:39–41) and mocked (chief priests, Matthew 27:43), and that soldiers would gamble for His robe (John 19:24). It was prophesied that Messiah would be buried in a rich man's grave (Isaiah 53:9) and that He would rise on the third day (Matthew 12:40). Jesus fulfilled them each.

Second, concerning the tomb of Jesus, Pilate and the Sanhedrin took preemptive measures in three ways to prevent a resurrection hoax. First, Roman soldiers (elite trained fighting men of the highest order) guarded Jesus' tomb. Second, a massive stone (weighing one and a half to two tons) sealed Jesus' tomb. Third, the Roman seal, which stood for the power and authority of the Roman Empire, was affixed to the tomb. Automatic execution by crucifixion upside down would be the lot of anyone who broke the seal. What could be done was done competently to avert the theft of Jesus' body.

With these safeguards, it was impossible for the disciples or any others to have stolen the body of Jesus. Note that the disciples' behavior and eventual death for Christ indicate that they didn't steal the body. Tradition and early Christian historians state that most of the disciples died a martyr's death for belief in Jesus' resurrection. Had they stolen the body and invented the lie that He was alive, they would have suffered and died for a lie, which is preposterous.[293] "There was no incentive to steal Jesus' body and lie about it. There was nothing to gain and everything to lose."[294]

*There is reason to believe in the resurrection of Christ because of what happened during it.*

1) The stone was supernaturally rolled away, not to let Jesus out, but for us to look in.

2) The linen wrappings placed on the body of Jesus were found in the tomb in a fashion that indicated Jesus passed through them. Had thieves taken Jesus' body, these wrappings would have been in disarray.

3) The appearance of the two angels to Mary Magdalene and the other women at the empty tomb.

4) Jesus' appearance and words to Mary Magdalene outside the tomb.

*There is reason to believe in the resurrection of Christ because of what happened after it.*

1) The plot (the propagation of the lie by the soldiers that guarded the tomb that the disciples stole Jesus' body), which the Sanhedrin quickly devised to conceal the truth of Jesus' resurrection, helped to confirm it.

2) For days after the resurrection, friends and enemies testified that they saw Jesus alive.[295] There were more than 1,500 eyewitnesses to His resurrection (1 Corinthians 15:3–6), including:

• Mary Magdalene (John 20:11–18)

• Other women (Matthew 28:9, 10)

• Peter (Luke 24:34; 1 Corinthians 15:5)

• Two disciples on the Emmaus Road (Luke 24:13–35)

• Ten disciples (Luke 24:36; John 20:19–25)

- Thomas (John 20:26–31)

- Seven disciples on the Sea of Galilee (John 21:1–25)

- The eleven disciples at the giving of the Great Commission (Matthew 28:16–20)

- The five hundred [only men were numbered in New Testament times; factoring in women and children, this number could easily have exceeded 1,500] (1 Corinthians 15:6)

- James (1 Corinthians 15:7)

- Those at His ascension (Acts 1:9–10)

- Stephen (Acts 7:55–60)

- Paul on the way to Damascus (Acts 9:3–6)

- Paul in the Temple (Acts 22:17–21)

- Paul on the ship going to Rome (Acts 23:11)

- John (Revelation 1:10–18)

"The appearances of Jesus," says Michael Green, "are as well authenticated as anything in antiquity....There can be no rational doubt that they occurred." Said Spurgeon, "The resurrection of Jesus Christ from the dead is one of the best-attested facts on record. There were so many witnesses to behold it that if we do in the least degree receive the credibility of men's testimonies, we cannot, and we dare not doubt that Jesus rose from the dead."

*There is reason to believe in the resurrection of Christ on account of what happened because of it.*

1) A change was manifested in the disciples. Before the resurrection, they were fearful and cowardly. Still, after seeing the risen Christ, they were bold and courageous in proclaiming the Gospel for which they would ultimately be executed (all died a martyr's death save one). Note, people don't die for what they know is a hoax or lie.

2) A change was manifested in the half-brother of Jesus, James. He was not a believer until the resurrected Christ appeared to him (1 Corinthians 15:7). Eventually, James became a leader in the

Jerusalem church and later a martyr. Michael Licona states, "James was so thoroughly convinced of Jesus' Messiahship because of the resurrection that he died as a martyr, as both Christian and non-Christian sources attest."[296]

Lee Strobel asked Licona, "In the end, do you think James' conversion is significant evidence for the resurrection?"

He stated frankly, "Absolutely, yes, I do."[297]

3) A change was manifested in thousands outside the disciple band. Christian philosopher J. P. Moreland states that within weeks of the resurrection, a community of at least ten thousand Jews gave up the very sociological and theological traditions that had given them their national identity.[298]

4) The day of worship was changed to the first day of the week. The early church believed in the resurrection of Christ so much that they engaged in corporate worship on Sunday to celebrate it—something the Christian church still does.

5) A change occurs each time a sinner trusts Christ as Lord and Savior. E. Y. Mullins stated above, "The morally transformed man proves the deity of Christ, proves His presence [and proves the resurrection] in religious experience because no man has moral resources to transform himself. It proves the deity of Christ because when the sinner turns to Christ, he gets the response. Christ invites him, and he responds. He calls, and Christ answers. In his outward life, a new force begins to work, a new design, a new labor working to an end. But especially within is there Another, one with whom there is fellowship, to whom he becomes passionately devoted, whose presence is happiness and whose absence is sorrow."[299]

Again, as Billy Graham said above, "There is more evidence that Jesus rose from the dead than there is that Julius Caesar ever lived or that Alexander the Great died at the age of thirty-three."[300]

### The Belief in the Substitutionary Death of Christ for Man's Sin

"Christ died once for our sins. An innocent person died for those who are guilty. Christ did this to bring you to God, when his body was put to death and his spirit was made alive" (1 Peter 3:18 CEV).

*The Substitutionary Death of Christ for man's sin was planned by God.* Christ's substitutionary death was designed and prepared before the foundation of the world. Peter says, "For ye know that ye were not redeemed with corruptible things, such as silver and gold, from your vain way of living which ye received by tradition from your fathers, but with the precious blood of Christ, as of a lamb without blemish and without spot, who verily was foreordained before the foundation of the world, but was manifest in these last times for you" (1 Peter 1:18–20 KJ21). Long before God hung the sun, moon, stars, and planets in place, long before He created man, He ordained that His only Son, Jesus, would leave Heaven to come to Earth to die on the Cross to atone for man's sin to provide forgiveness of sin and eternal life. Spurgeon states, "Throughout the Old Testament, this was always the idea of a sin-offering—that of a perfect victim; without offense on its own account, taking the place of the offender; the transference of the offender's sin to that victim, and that expiation in the person of the victim for the sin done by another."

*The Substitutionary Death of Christ for man's sin was acceptable to God.* Who might qualify to die as man's substitute for payment of the debt of sin against our holy God?

1) The substitute had to be without sin. Paul says, "For he [God] hath made him [Jesus] to be sin for us, who knew no sin; that we might be made the righteousness of God in him" (2 Corinthians 5:21). Jesus, the lamb of God without spot or blemish, was alone worthy of dying in man's place.

2) The substitute had to be capable of paying that kind of debt. Luke said, "Jesus is the only One who can save people. No one else in the world is able to save us" (Acts 4:12 ICB).

3) The substitute had to be willing to pay the debt. He had to be obedient to the death of the Cross, to give his life to cancel man's debt of sin owed to God. Paul states, "And being found in the fashion of a man, He [Jesus] humbled Himself and became obedient unto death—even the death of the cross" (Philippians 2:8 KJ21). Jesus said, "No one can take my life from me. I sacrifice it voluntarily. For

116

I have the authority to lay it down when I want to and also to take it up again" (John 10:18 NLT).

4) The substitute had to be victorious over death. Christ's resurrection proves God accepted His payment at Calvary to fully settle man's sin debt. Paul says, "He was handed over to die because of our sins, and he was raised to life to make us right with God" (Romans 4:25 NLT). Of Himself, Jesus said, "I am he that liveth, and was dead; and, behold, I am alive for evermore, Amen; and have the keys of hell and of death" (Revelation 1:18). See 1 Corinthians 15:56–57.

Christ met all the requirements of a worthy substitute, satisfying the just demands of God's judgment for man's sin (none other could). Christ, the *Just,* took the place of man, the *unjust*; He, the *sinless,* took the place of man, the *sinful*, paying the price (debt) for man's sin (substitutionary death), canceling sin's consequence (eternal punishment in Hell). Nothing short of Jesus' shed blood and death at Calvary (not His perfection, example, teaching, suffering, or works) could cancel man's sin debt. "Without shedding of blood is no remission" (Hebrews 9:22). "Neither by the blood of goats and calves, but by his own blood he entered in once into the holy place, having obtained eternal redemption for us" (Hebrews 9:12).

Nothing can for sin atone:
    Nothing but the blood of Jesus.
Naught of good that I have done:
    Nothing but the blood of Jesus.

~Robert Lowry (1876)

Thomas Brooks said, "Our sins are debts that none can pay but Christ. It is not our tears, but His blood; it is not our sighs, but His sufferings, that can testify for our sins. Christ must pay all, or we are prisoners forever." Anselm said, "The debt was so great that while man alone owed it, only God could pay it." And praise be to His name, He did, as we see in John 1:14.

*The Substitutionary Death of Christ for man's sin was once and for all.* Christ's death for man's sin never needs repeating. Paul says, "The death he died, he died to sin once for all" (Romans 6:10 NIV).

The writer of Hebrews states, "Our sins are washed away and we are made clean because Christ gave His own body as a gift to God. He did this once for all time" (Hebrews 10:10 NLV). The work performed by Christ on the Cross 2,000 years ago to purchase man's redemption is just as effectual as when it was wrought and shall be until the end of the world. The blood of Jesus will never lose its power to atone for man's sin.

Spurgeon says, "The everlasting result of this effectual carrying out of the will of God is that now God regards His people's sin as expiated and their persons as sanctified. Offered, and its efficacy abides forever."[301]

*The Substitutionary Death of Christ for man's sin was universal in scope.* Jesus' atoning death was on behalf of all mankind. John says, "He is the one who took God's wrath against our sins upon himself and brought us into fellowship with God; and he is the forgiveness for our sins, and not only ours but all the world's" (1 John 2:2 TLB). Regardless of man's religious estate or locale, Paul says unequivocally that the Son of God gave Himself for us (Galatians 2:20). The prophet Isaiah, peering down through the centuries, beheld Christ's death at Calvary and cried out, "But He was wounded for our transgressions; He was bruised for our iniquities. The chastisement of our peace was upon Him, and with His stripes, we are healed. All we like sheep have gone astray; we have turned every one to his own way; and the Lord hath laid on Him the iniquity of us all" (Isaiah 53:5–6 KJ21).

*The Substitutionary Death of Christ for man's sin was inclusive.* Paul asserts, "Because we broke God's laws, we owed a debt—a debt that listed all the rules we failed to follow. But God forgave us of that debt. He took it away and nailed it to the cross" (Colossians 2:14 ERV). Christ at Calvary wiped out (blotted out, erased) man's every sin (past, present, future) and our debt against God.

My sin, oh, the bliss of this glorious thought!
My sin, not in part but the whole
Is nailed to the cross, and I bear it no more.

118

*The Substitutionary Death of Christ for man's sin was and is soul-saving.* Paul states, "In whom we have redemption through his blood, even the forgiveness of sins" (Colossians 1:14). Watchman Nee said, "By accepting His death as our death, we enter into this union with the Lord." "Christ took our sins and the sins of the whole world," wrote Martin Luther, "as well as the Father's wrath on His shoulders, and He has drowned them both in himself so that we are thereby reconciled to God and become completely righteous." Peter states, "Christ carried our sins in his body on the cross so that freed from our sins, we could live a life that has God's approval. His wounds have healed you" (1 Peter 2:24 GW). Though Christ's death is efficient and sufficient to save unto the uttermost, it only avails for him who accepts it by faith (Hebrews 7:25). See Ephesians 2:8–9.

During the Civil War, there was a band of organized outlaws in the Midwest called Quantrell's Raiders. The terror they created and the robbing they did caused people in Kansas to form a militia to hunt them down with orders to execute all that could be found. Soon, a group of these desperados was captured in Iowa. They were lined up in a trench awaiting execution by a firing squad when a young man cried out, "Wait! Wait!" Addressing the commanding officer, he pointed to a man waiting to be shot and said, "Let that man go free. He has a wife and babies and is needed at home. Let me take his place." The commanding officer ordered the replacement of the condemned man with the volunteer. The one walked away free; the other fell dead before the firing squad.

In time, the redeemed man returned to claim the young man's body. He placed it on a mule and took it to a cemetery near Kansas City for a proper burial. He marked it with a crude wooden slab. Later, he erected a 15-foot marble monument inscribed with the words:

*SACRED TO THE MEMORY OF WILLIE LEE*
*HE TOOK MY PLACE IN THE LINE*
*HE DIED FOR ME*

The redeemed may say of Christ, "Sacred to the memory of Jesus Christ. He took my place on the Cross and gave His life so I might go free and have life abundantly and eternally."

### The Belief in the Bible Doctrine of Hell

"Multitudes who sleep in the dust of the earth will awake: some to everlasting life, others to shame and everlasting contempt" (Daniel 12:2 NIV). Why believe in the reality of Hell?

*The Witness of the Savior.* Christ's unequivocal attestation to the fact of Hell is the surest of all proofs of its existence. He taught it, confirmed it, wept over it, warned about it, and died on the Cross to keep men out of it. Christ spoke of Hell more than any other biblical writer.

Robert W. Yarbrough said, "If His (Jesus') words about Hell are set aside, then nearly all of His teachings must be neutralized."[302] D. L. Moody asserts, "The same Christ that tells of Heaven with all of its glories tells us of Hell with all of its horrors." Spurgeon remarked, "It is a very remarkable fact that no inspired preacher of whom we have any record ever uttered such terrible words concerning the destiny of the lost as our Lord Jesus Christ."[303]

Jesus reveals the actuality of Hell and describes it (a photograph of Hell) in the story of the rich man and Lazarus (Luke 16:19–31).

1) *Hell is a Place* (Luke 16:28). It is a literal place, not a state of mind. The rich man didn't want his brothers to 'also come to this place of torment.'

2) *Hell is a place of Pain* (Luke 16:23–24). Physical and mental torment unimaginable, of varying degrees, will be experienced in Hell (Matthew 10:15; 11:22, 24; Mark 6:11; Hebrews 10:29).

3) *Hell is a place of Passion* (Luke 16:24). Insatiable appetites and desires plague the inhabitants of Hell forever.

4) *Hell is a place of Parting* (Luke 16:26). The unsaved, eternally separated from the believers, are shut up with the vilest companions.

5) *Hell is a place of Prayer* (Luke 16: 24, 27). Pleas are made, begging for merciful relief from the suffering experienced and for

warning to be given to family and friends not to go there—but the praying is futile.

6) *Hell is a place of Permanence* (Luke 16:26). Hell has no exits. There is no way out of its domain, so its inhabitants are without hope of escape or rescue. One can purchase a shirt in Hell, Michigan, which states, "I've been to Hell and back." But none that go to the eternal Hell ever come back.

A. W. Pink states, "The doom of those who shall be cast into the Lake of Fire is irrevocable and final. Many independent considerations prove this. Forgiveness of sins is limited to life on this earth. Once the sinner passes out of this world, there remaineth 'no more sacrifice for sins.' The fact that at death the soul of the wicked goes at once into the 'furnace of fire' (Matthew 13:42) witnesses to the fixity of his future state."[304] There are no backdoors out of Hell. The worst part of Hell is that *it is a place where God is not!*

In the Sermon on the Mount (Matthew 5–7), Jesus told of the existence and judgment of Hell no fewer than six times. In Matthew 10:28, Jesus warned about the One who can destroy both body and soul in Hell. In Mark 9:43 of the NIV, Jesus spoke of Hell as a place "where the fire never goes out." Furthermore, in Matthew 25:41, Jesus said that Hell was "prepared for the devil and his angels," revealing for whom the abode was initially intended (not man, but Satan and the demons).

In the Olivet Discourse, Jesus spoke of Hell in the parables of the servants (Matthew 24:45–51), talents (Matthew 25:14–30), and the lesson of the sheep and goats (Matthew 25:31–46). In Matthew 13:49–50, Jesus said, "This is how it will be at the end of the age. The angels will come and separate the wicked from the righteous and throw them into the blazing furnace, where there will be weeping and gnashing of teeth" (NIV). Did Jesus lie or tell the truth of the torment that awaits the unrepentant at death in Hell? Since He can't lie (Hebrews 6:18), bank on it: Hell is for real.

*The Witness of the Apostles and Prophets.* The apostle Paul testified to Hell as a place of eternal destruction: "These people will pay the penalty and endure the punishment of everlasting destruction, banished from the presence of the Lord and from the glory of His power" (2 Thessalonians 1:9 AMP). Jude describes Hell as "the blackness of darkness forever" (Jude 13). Utter blackness makes relationships impossible in Hell.

C. S. Lewis declared Hell is a place of "nothing but yourself for all eternity!" The inhabitants of Hell know only isolation and loneliness; no friendships or fellowship exist. Peter argues that if God spared not the angels that sinned but "sent them to Hell, putting them in chains of darkness to be held for judgment" (2 Peter 2:4 NIV), how much more so will He the unrepentant among men. Of Hell, John said, "And the devil that deceived them was cast into the lake of fire and brimstone, where the beast and the false prophet are, and shall be tormented day and night forever and ever....And whosoever was not found written in the book of life was cast into the lake of fire" (Revelation 20:10, 15).

Isaiah records the words of the Lord about eternal destruction in Hell: "For as the new heavens and the new earth, which I will make, shall remain before me, saith the Lord, so shall your seed and your name remain. And it shall come to pass, that from one new moon to another, and from one sabbath to another, shall all flesh come to worship before me, saith the LORD. And they shall go forth, and look upon the carcasses of the men that have transgressed against me: for their worm shall not die, neither shall their fire be quenched; and they shall be an abhorring unto all flesh" (Isaiah 66:22–24). Daniel testifies to the reality of Hell, saying, "And many of them that sleep in the dust of the earth shall awake, some to everlasting life, and some to shame and everlasting contempt" (Daniel 12:2).

*The witness of the Scriptures.* R. G. Lee asserts, "No man can go to the New Testament and not find Hell in the New Testament."[305] J. C. Ryle said, "Disbelieve Hell, and you unscrew, unsettle, and unpin everything in Scripture." The whole of theological doctrine taught in the Scriptures—the moral attributes of God, His holiness, His justice and fairness—is interwoven on the premise of the existence of Hell.[306] J. I. Packer states, "Universalism [there is no Hell; all go to Heaven] does not stand up to biblical examination. Its sunny optimism may be reassuring and comfortable, but it wholly misses the tragic quality of human sin, human unbelief, and human death set forth in the Bible. Universalism reinvents, and thereby distorts, biblical teaching about God and salvation."[307] Anti-universalist teaching in the New Testament, states O. C. Quick, is "conclusive."[308]

J. C. Ryle says, "The Scripture has spoken plainly and fully on the subject of Hell. The same Bible which teaches that God in mercy and compassion sent Christ to die for sinners also teaches that God hates sin and must from His very nature punish all who cleave to sin or refuse the salvation He has provided."[309] The Holy Scriptures' documentation and description of Hell are plenteous. Hell is a lake of fire (Revelation 20:15); a place of everlasting punishment (Matthew 25:46); a bottomless pit (Revelation 20:1); and a place of permeating darkness (Jude 13); a place prepared for the devil and his angels (Matthew 25:41); a place of weeping and gnashing of teeth (Matthew 13:42); a place where there is no rest day or night (Revelation 14:11); a place of unquenchable fire (Mark 9:48); a place that is separated from the presence of God and the glory of His power (2 Thessalonians 1:8–9); a place where there is no repentance (Matthew 12:32); a place filled with blasphemies against God (Revelation 16:11); a place where its inhabitants want loved ones warned not to come (Luke 16:28); a place of intolerable memory and remorse (Luke 16:25); a place which is the eternal home of murderers, the immoral, liars, the corrupt, cowards, and unbelievers (Revelation 21:8); a place of eternal damnation (Mark 3:29).

The bottom line? Spurgeon says, "If you doubt the punishment of the future state, doubt the inspiration of Scripture at once, for to doubt one and hold the other is impossible. Do not so violate your own conscience as to dream of sin's escaping punishment. If you should persuade yourself to doubt the existence of Hell, your doubting it will not quench its fires. If there be no Hell hereafter, I am as well off as you are, but if there be, where will you be?"[310]

*The Witness of the Cross.* To deny Hell is to reject the purpose of the suffering and death of Christ at Calvary. Unequivocally the Scriptures state that Jesus' death was a substitutionary death for sinful man as payment for sins committed to avert eternal punishment in a place where there is weeping and gnashing of teeth and the fire is not quenched (1 Peter 3:18; Romans 6:23). Elbert Munsey asserts, "The existence of the atonement is evidence there is a state of future punishment. If there is no state of future punishment, the atonement is at once perceived to be a supererogation—a something superinduced upon the grand system of God's moral government, for the existence of which there can be no sensible reason assigned."[311]

Spurgeon reasons, "Brethren, if the wrath of God be a mere trifle, there was no need of a Savior to deliver us; it was as well to have let so small a matter take its course?"[312] R. G. Lee argues, "If a man accepts the atonement of Christ—how can he doubt the dogma of Hell?"

*The Witness of the Conscience.* "The conscience of every sinner," says Spurgeon, "tells him that there will be a wrath to come. I do not mean that the conscience of the sinner tells him what kind of punishment it will be or dictates to him its duration, but we know from facts that dying men who have lived in impenitence have often exhibited fears that are not to be accounted for except upon the supposition that the shadow of a terrible doom had cast itself upon their minds."[313]

An example of such a troubling conscience was Sir Thomas Scott, who said upon his deathbed, "Until this moment, I thought there was neither a God nor a Hell. Now I know and feel that there are both, and I am doomed to perdition by the just judgment of the Almighty."

*There is only one way to avoid Hell at death.* Spurgeon said, "Sin and Hell are married unless repentance proclaims the divorce."[314] Man must look to Christ for the cleansing and forgiveness of sin and turn to Him (repentance) in complete trust for salvation (saving grace and mercy—Ephesians 2:8–9). "The Lord is not slow about keeping His promise as some people think. He is waiting for you. The Lord does not want any person to be punished forever. He wants all people to be sorry for their sins and turn from them" (2 Peter 3:9 NLV).

Hell is truth seen too late by most. Jesus said, "Enter through the narrow gate. The gate is wide and the road is wide that leads to hell, and many people enter through that gate. But the gate is small and the road is narrow that leads to true life. Only a few people find that road" (Matthew 7:13–14 NCV).

## The Belief in the Place called Heaven

"I go to prepare a place for you" (John 14:2). Heaven is a place of the eternal abode of God (Isaiah 57:15), angels (Mark 13:32), and the saints (Revelation 7:14–15). It's a place of absolute righteousness, happiness, rest, worship, reunion, rewards, and service, where pain, sorrow, and death do not exist.

Belief in the actuality of Heaven is founded upon unshakeable attestations.

*The attestation of Holy Scripture.* Hundreds of fulfilled prophecies, archaeological digs, and extrabiblical sources authenticate the Bible as God's truthful and trustworthy Word. Its references to Heaven (about 550 times) bear proof of its actuality (2 Peter 1:19).

In 2 Corinthians 5:1–8 Paul states that the believer at death acquires a glorified body ("house")—that the new house, unlike the present one of flesh and blood, is eternal, permanent (2 Corinthians 5:1b); that a transformation awaits at death—mortality will be swallowed up by immortality (2 Corinthians 5:3–4); that the soul immediately at death is in the presence of the Lord—there is no soul sleep in the grave awaiting the rapture of the church (2 Corinthians 5:8); and that the believer will dwell forever in a Heavenly Home— "a house not made with hands, eternal in the heavens" (2 Corinthians 5:1b).

John says, "He will wipe away every tear from their eyes, and death shall be no more, neither shall there be mourning, nor crying, nor pain anymore, for the former things have passed away. And he who was seated on the throne said, 'Behold, I am making all things new.' Also, he said, 'Write this down, for these words are trustworthy and true.'" (Revelation 21:4–5 ESV).

This promise of Heaven contains one of my favorite lines in the Bible: "These words are *trustworthy and true*." Everything in John's vision on the Isle of Patmos of the Celestial City (Heaven) is true and reliable. Saith John Gill, "These words are true and faithful; both what he had said, and was about to say; they were 'true,' because they came from God, who cannot lie, and 'faithful' because they would be punctually and exactly fulfilled."

David said, "I will dwell in the house of the LORD forever" (Psalm 23:6). "This language implies the assurance, on his part, of the existence of a state of future blessedness."[315] Job declared, "After my skin has been destroyed, yet in my flesh I will see God; I myself will see him with my own eyes—I, and not another" (Job 19:26–27 NIV). Job expressed the certainty of belief in a bodily resurrection, at which time he would see his Redeemer with "my own eyes" and share fellowship with Him. What a picture of Heaven!

Daniel said, "Many people who have already died will live again. Some of them will wake up to have life forever, but some will wake up to find shame and disgrace forever" (Daniel 12:2 NCV). Daniel testifies to two resurrections—one for the redeemed unto life eternal (Heaven) and the second for the lost unto everlasting shame and disgrace (Hell). Solomon states about the future life that "the righteous hath hope in his death" (Proverbs 14:32). The believers' hope is the Blessed Hope of Heaven that God promised (1 Peter 1:3–6). Matthew Henry said of the godly, "He has hope in his death of a happiness on the other side death, of better things in another world than ever he had in this."[316]

*The attestation of Jesus.* Jesus said, "In my Father's house are many mansions: if it were not so, I would have told you" (John 14:2). This promise of Heaven contains another of my favorite lines in the Bible: "If it were not so, I would have told you." That is, "If there were no Heaven, if you were clinging to nothing more than a pipe dream about it, if your expectations about it were mistaken, I would have told you. If there were no Heaven with its mansions, streets of gold and walls of Jasper, reunion, rest and peace, I would not have told you that there was, only to let you be deceived and disappointed." Jesus came into the world to reveal and speak the truth, and did without exception: "To this end was I born, and for this cause came I into the world, that I should bear witness unto the truth" (John 18:37). See Ephesians 4:21 and John 14:6. "Like God, Jesus needed no one else to support his assertions of truth, except to refer to himself."[317]

*The attestation of the faithfulness of God to keep His Promises.* "In hope of eternal life, which God, that cannot lie, promised before the world began" (Titus 1:2). A belief in Heaven is founded upon God's reliability to keep His promises. He promised to give eternal life in Heaven to repentant sinners before the foundation of the world. And His Word is trustworthy and true. Seeing that God cannot lie, embrace His promise of Heaven with joy, anticipation, and confidence.

*The attestation of the imprint of Heaven within man.* "Also he hath set eternity in their heart" (Ecclesiastes 3:11 ASV). A belief in Heaven is founded upon the inscription of this divine truth in man's soul. God has stamped the heart with the awareness and desire of Heaven. When we listen to our heart, it says, "I am a stranger here, within a foreign land; My home is far away, upon a golden strand." It says, "For here we have no continuing city, but we seek one to come" (Hebrews 13:14 KJ21). "For our citizenship is in heaven, and from there we eagerly wait for the Savior" (Philippians 3:20 TLV). It says, we look "for a city which hath foundations, whose builder and maker is God" (Hebrews 11:10). And our heart sings, "We shall see the King someday; we will sing and shout someday. Gathered around the Throne, we shall see the King someday."

A pastor noted a little boy with arms extended toward the sky holding a string tightly in his hands. He inquired, "What are you doing here, my little friend?"

"Flying my kite, sir," he replied.

"Flying your kite!" exclaimed the pastor. "I can see no kite; you can see none."

The boy replied, "I know, sir. I cannot see it, but I know it is there, for *I feel its pull.*"

Though Heaven is not visible from our vantage point, we know it is there, for we feel its pull! "For in this we groan, earnestly desiring to be clothed upon with our house which is from heaven" (2 Corinthians 5:2). See Romans 8:23.

*The attestation of the resurrection of Christ.* "But Christ has been raised to life! And he makes us certain that others will also be raised to life" (1 Corinthians 15:20 CEV). A belief in Heaven is founded upon the resurrection of Christ. His crucifixion and subsequent resurrection thwarted sin and death's power and opened the door to Heaven for repentant sinners. He said, "Because I live, ye shall live also" (John 14:19).

Paul says of the believers' resurrection to Heaven, "It will happen suddenly, quicker than the blink of an eye. At the sound of the last trumpet the dead will be raised. We will all be changed, so we will never die again. Our dead and decaying bodies will be changed into bodies that won't die or decay. The bodies we now have are weak and can die. But they will be changed into bodies that are eternal" (1 Corinthians 15:52–54 CEV). See Romans 6:6.

J. C. Ryle writes, "There is a resurrection after death. Let this never be forgotten. The life that we live here in the flesh is not all. The visible world around us is not the only world with which we have to do. All is not over when the last breath is drawn and men and women are carried to their long home in the grave. The trumpet shall one day sound and the dead shall be raised incorruptible. Let us cling to it [this hope] firmly and never let it go." The surety of the believer's future life is found in the angel's words to the two Marys on that first Easter morning, "He is not here: for he is risen, as he said" (Matthew 28:6).

When thou didst overcome the sharpness of death,
Thou didst open the kingdom of Heaven unto all believers.
Thou sittest at the right hand of God in the glory of the Father.
~*Te Deum* (Latin hymn)

*The attestation of the Holy Spirit's presence in the redeemed.*

1) The Holy Spirit's presence within believers is God's pledge that someday they will live with Him in Heaven. "The Spirit is God's guarantee that he will give us the inheritance he promised and that he has purchased us to be his own people" (Ephesians 1:14 NLT). William Barclay comments, "What Paul is saying is that the experience of the Holy Spirit which we have in this world is a foretaste of the blessedness of Heaven, and it is the guarantee that someday we will enter into full possession of the blessedness of

God."[318] Said Matthew Henry, "The present graces and comforts of the Spirit are earnests [down-payment] of ever-lasting grace and comfort."[319] Paul also refers to the Holy Spirit as God's pledge of future life in 2 Corinthians 5:5.

2) The Holy Spirit bears witness to the believer of a future Home in Heaven. Commenting on Paul's confidence in Heaven, Alan Redpath says, "He knew God so intimately, not as a stranger but as a Father, because he believed in Christ. He was a member of God's great family, and he knew that the Father one day would welcome him home. You see, this man was sure, and he had grounds for his confidence because Father, Son, and Holy Spirit witnessed to him of the absolute assurance that one day he would be with Jesus."[320] Paul's certainty of eternal life in Heaven was rooted in Christ's resurrection (John 2:19), and the witness of the Spirit deepened that certainty.

*The way to Heaven.* Billy Graham said, "Only one answer will give a person the certain privilege, the joy, of entering Heaven. 'Because I have believed in Jesus Christ and accepted him as my Savior.'"[321] See John 10:9.

Here in this world, He bids us come;
There in the next, He shall bid us welcome.

~John Donne

### The Belief in the Second Coming of Christ

When the Bible speaks of the Second Coming of Christ, it does not refer to the coming of the Holy Spirit or His coming in the sinner's salvation or coming for the saint at death. It addresses the physical and visible bodily return of Christ to take the redeemed of God to their Home in Heaven. The angels said to the watching disciples, "This same Jesus, who is taken up from you into Heaven, shall so come in like manner as ye have seen Him go into Heaven" (Acts 1:11 KJ21). Of the doctrine of the Second Coming, W. A. Criswell states, "There is no truth more certain in the entire Bible." On what basis may man believe that Christ will soon bodily and visibly return to earth?

*The past fulfillment of the prophecies about Christ is a reason to believe the prophecies of His return.* Christ fulfilled, among others, the Virgin birth prophecy (Isaiah 7:14), the Bethlehem prophecy (Micah 5:2), the Davidic prophecy (Jeremiah 23:5–6), the Crucifixion prophecy (Psalm 22:13–18), the rich man burial prophecy (Isaiah 53:9) and the Resurrection prophecy (John 2:19). Christ's unquestionable fulfillment of all these prophecies bears witness to His authority, ability, and faithfulness to fulfill the prophecy of His Second Coming.

*The authority of the Holy Scriptures.* The Bible over-whelmingly substantiates the return of Christ and provides it with credible documentation. By a ratio of eight to one, references to the Second Coming of Christ in the Bible outnumber those to the First Coming. Note, the term Second Coming is not used in the Bible; it is always referred to as *the* coming, *the* appearing, *the* presence of the Lord.[322] Francis Dixon says, "Scripture knows no first coming without a second coming. The two comings are entwined, interwoven, and inseparable in the prophetic Word."[323]

It is attested by scholars that the prophecy of the Second Coming of Christ is mentioned no less than 1200 times in the Old Testament[324] and is found in at least seventeen of its books. Daniel prophesied about it. "I saw in the night visions, and, behold, one like the Son of man came with the clouds of heaven, and came to the Ancient of days, and they brought him near before him. And there was given him dominion, and glory, and a kingdom, that all people, nations, and languages, should serve him: his dominion is an everlasting dominion, which shall not pass away, and his kingdom that which shall not be destroyed" (Daniel 7:13–14).

Enoch testified of it. "And Enoch also, the seventh from Adam, prophesied of these, saying, "Behold, the Lord cometh with ten thousand of His saints To execute judgment upon all, and to convince all that are ungodly among them of all their ungodly deeds which they have ungodly committed, and of all their hard speeches which ungodly sinners have spoken against him" (Jude 14–15 KJ21). Isaiah declared it, describing the peace on earth under His rule (Isaiah 11:1–10). The psalmist pronounced it. "For he comes, for he comes to judge the earth" (Psalm 96:13 ESV).

Zechariah taught it. "On that day his feet shall stand on the Mount of Olives that lies before Jerusalem on the east, and the Mount of Olives shall be split in two from east to west by a very wide valley, so that one half of the Mount shall move northward, and the other half southward" (Zechariah 14:4 ESV). The prophet continues, "The Lord will become king over all the earth; on that day the Lord will be one and his name one" (Zechariah 14:9 RSV).

In the New Testament, there are 318 references that directly or indirectly refer to the second coming of Christ[325]; one verse in every thirty refers to it, and seven out of every ten chapters mention it. Only two books, Philemon and 3 John, are silent about it.[326]

The two angels at the Ascension proclaimed it. "Ye men of Galilee, why stand ye gazing up into heaven? this same Jesus, which is taken up from you into heaven, shall so come in like manner as ye have seen him go into heaven" (Acts 1:11). Note, it was an angel(s) that announced Christ's first coming to the lowly shepherds in the fields (Luke 2:8–10), His resurrection to the women at the tomb (Matthew 28:6), the promise of the second coming to the disciples on the Mount of Ascension (Acts 1:11), and it will be an archangel that adds his voice and trumpet blasting to that of the command of Christ announcing His return (1 Thessalonians 4:16–17; 1 Corinthians 15:52).

Paul believed it. "For the Lord himself shall descend from heaven with a shout, with the voice of the archangel, and with the trump of God: and the dead in Christ shall rise first: Then we which are alive and remain shall be caught up together with them in the clouds, to meet the Lord in the air: and so shall we ever be with the Lord" (1 Thessalonians 4:16–17). See 1 Corinthians 15:51–58; 1 Thessalonians 3:13; 5:1–4; 2 Thessalonians 1:7–8, 10; 2 Timothy 4:1, 8; Titus 2:13.

The Gospels teach it. The Olivet Discourse vividly and explicitly describes the Second Coming of Christ (Matthew 24–25; Mark 13; Luke 21:5–38).

The author of Hebrews emphasized it. "So Christ was once offered to bear the sins of many; and unto them that look for him shall he appear the second time without sin unto salvation" (Hebrews 9:28). James affirmed it. "Be patient therefore, brethren, unto the coming of the Lord. Behold, the husbandman waiteth for the precious fruit of the earth, and hath long patience for it, until he receive the early and latter rain. Be ye also patient; stablish your hearts: for the coming of the Lord draweth nigh" (James 5:7–8).

Peter asserts it. "And when the Chief Shepherd shall appear, ye shall receive a crown of glory that fadeth not away" (1 Peter 5:4). See 1 Peter 1:10–11; 2 Peter 3:3–4. John amplifies it. "Beloved, now are we the sons of God, and it doth not yet appear what we shall be: but we know that, when he shall appear, we shall be like him; for we shall see him as he is" (1 John 3:2). See 1 John 2:28. The Book of Revelation, authored by John, reveals Christ's return. Revelation 19 explicitly details that glorious event.

*The prophecy of Christ's return is interwoven with every fundamental doctrine of the Scripture.* I. M. Haldeman asserts, "Not only is the doctrine (Second Coming) the predominantly mentioned one of the Bible; it is also the one bound up with every other doctrine of the Word of God—so bound up that it cannot be neglected without disaster to the whole body of truth."[327] Agreeing, Spurgeon states, "Make you sure of this, that the whole drama of redemption cannot be perfected without this last act of the coming of the King. The complete history of Paradise Regained requires that the New Jerusalem should come down from God out of Heaven, prepared as a bride adorned for her husband, and it also requires that the heavenly Bridegroom should come riding forth on His white horse, conquering and to conquer, King of kings and Lord of lords, amidst the everlasting hallelujahs of saints and angels. It must be so."[328]

*The promise of Jesus.* Jesus unquestionably and dogmatically asserts that He will return. In John 14, the promise is stated in four words: "I will come back" (John 14:3 GNT). In Revelation 22, the promise of Christ's return is said three times in three verses: "Behold, I come quickly" (Revelation 22:7), "Behold, I come quickly" (Revelation 22:12), "Surely I come quickly" (Revelation 22:20). Christ spoke of His return 21 times.

W. A. Criswell asserts, "The infallibility, integrity, and moral authority of the Son of God are bound up in His keeping that word that He will come again."[329] And He will. Christ's word is dependable and trustworthy. What He says always happens. Note, of His Second Advent, He stated, "If it were not so, I would have told you." "God is not a man, that he should lie" (Numbers 23:19). Christians believe He is coming again because He said so.

Christ promised to return soon. "In a little while you will see Me no more, and then after a little while you will see Me" (John 16:16 NIV). His timetable is different from man's; a thousand years to Him is as a day (2 Peter 3:8). Nothing precludes His return to usher His children Home (Matthew 24:44). "Blessed are those servants, whom the lord when he cometh shall find watching" (Luke 12:37).

To watch for His coming is to live in expectancy and readiness for it. Christ promised to reward him who looks for His appearing. "Blessed" are they that look for the Lord's return. "Every man that hath this hope in him purifieth himself, even as he is pure." "Blessednesses," says Spurgeon, "are heaped up one upon another in that state of heart in which a man is always looking for his Lord."[330] But a future reward awaits when He returns. "Now, a prize is waiting for me—the crown that will show I am right with God. The Lord, the judge who judges rightly, will give it to me on that Day. Yes, he will give it to me and to everyone else who is eagerly looking forward to his coming" (2 Timothy 4:8 ERV).

*The people to whom He made the promise to return believed Him.* People who knew Jesus well believed what He declared about coming back and lived in constant expectancy of it. And that belief impacted how they lived and served God. "And now, little children, abide in him; that, when he shall appear, we may have confidence, and not be ashamed before him at his coming" (1 John 2:28).

If another has *credible* reason to believe a matter to be truth, then their assurance can be the grounds for our belief to its validity. The promise of the Lord's return has not one person, but myriads that unitedly say, "For the Son of man shall come in the glory of his Father with his angels" (Matthew 16:27).

*The witness of the saints throughout history proclaimed His return.* Astute historians, theologians, and preachers who walked with God and studied the Word intensely substantiate the fact of Christ's return (Polycarp, Ignatius, Calvin, Luther, Spurgeon, Moody,

Graham, Criswell, Torrey, etc.). Their confidence in the return of Christ, although not proof of it, ought to bear weight in its acceptance.

*The testimony in the believer's heart about the return of Christ.* The Holy Spirit has placed within the believer's heart an anxious expectation ("Blessed Hope") and certainty of the return of Christ, prompting him to say with John, "Amen. Even so, come, Lord Jesus" (Revelation 22:20).

Despite scoffers and mockers of the Second Coming prophecy, as in Peter's day (2 Peter 3:3), the evidence is overwhelming. Christ will come to take His children Home to Heaven (2 Peter 3:10). That is unalterable. "Look up, and lift up your heads; for your redemption draweth nigh" (Luke 21:28). Saith Spurgeon, "Brethren and sisters, regard the object of our expectations! See the happiness which is promised us! Behold the Heaven which awaits us! Forget for a while your present cares; let all your difficulties and your sorrows vanish for a season, and live for a while in the future which is so certified by faithful promises that you may rejoice in it even now!"[331]

A little while! our Lord shall come,
    And we shall wander here no more;
He'll take us to our Father's home,
    Where He for us has gone before,
To dwell with Him, to see His face,
And sing the glories of His grace.

~James G. Deck

# A Soulwinning Challenge

## *From the Pen of Charles Haddon Spurgeon*

"If you but could stand by one death bed where a soul is taking its leap into the dark, if for once you could hear the cries of a spirit as it enters into the thick darkness which is to be its everlasting abode, if you could but have painted before your eyes in verity the last tremendous day and the multitudes on the left hand, if you could but gaze for a moment at the Heaven which your own children I fear may miss through your indifference, or if you could but look for a second upon the Hell to which multitudes of your neighbors are descending every day, surely you would go down on your knees saying, 'Forgive me, Great God, for all my past neglect, and from this hour cleanse me from the blood of souls by the blood of Jesus, and help me be instant in season and out of season in instructing my fellow man. Never from this day until I die may I neglect an opportunity of telling men how they may be saved.'"

From the sermon "Serving the Lord," August 15, 1869.

A charge to keep I have,
   A God to glorify,
A never-dying soul to save,
   And fit it for the sky.

~Charles Wesley (1762)

Endnotes

[1] Spurgeon, C. H. "Soul Winning." Sermon delivered 1869, Metropolitan Tabernacle.
[2] Spurgeon, C. H. *The Soul Winner.* Chapter: "Soul Saving Our One Business."
[3] Ibid., 9.
[4] Rice, John R. *The Soulwinner's Fire.* (Murfreesboro: Sword of the Lord, 1941), 8–9.
[5] Riley, W. B. *Seven New Testament Soul-Winners.* (Grand Rapids: Wm. B. Eerdmans Publ. Co., 1939), Chapter Four: "Ananias—The Skillful Soul-Winner."
[6] Spurgeon, C. H. "One Lost Sheep" (sermon). *Metropolitan Tabernacle Pulpit,* Volume 35, www.spurgeongems.org accessed December 1, 2013.
[7] Mullins, E. Y. *Talks on Soul Winning.* (Nashville, TN: The Sunday School Board of the Southern Baptist Convention, 1920), 11.
[8] Davis, George T. B. *Dwight L. Moody, the Man and His Mission.* (K. T. Boland, 1900), 119.
[9] Wilson, Raymond. *Jenner of George Street: Sydney's Soul-Winning Sailor.* (2000), 73.
[10] Ibid.
[11] Spurgeon, C. H. *Morning and Evening,* June 20 (Evening).
[12] Hunter, George III. *How to Reach Secular People.* (Nashville, TN: Abingdon Press, 1992), 53–54.
[13] Autrey, C. E. *You Can Win Souls.* (Nashville: Broadman Press, 1961), 6.
[14] Matthews, C. E. *Every Christian's Job.* (Nashville: Broadman Press, 1951), 35.
[15] Drummond, Lewis. *The Word of the Cross.* (Nashville: Broadman Press, 1992), 337.
[16] Murray, Andrew. *Working for God.* (New York, Chicago, Toronto: Fleming H. Revell, August 1901), Chapter 28.
[17] Spurgeon, C. H. "The Christian's Great Business." Sermon delivered September 7, 1873, Metropolitan Tabernacle.
[18] Edwards, Jonathan. *Distinguishing Marks of a Work of the Spirit of God,* 1741. Modern language courtesy of Archie Parrish. *The Spirit of Revival.* (Crossway Books, 2000), 82.
[19] Downey, Murray. *The Art of Soulwinning.* (Grand Rapids, MI: Baker Book House, 1957), 11.
[20] Bright, Bill. *The 10 Basic Steps Toward Christian Maturity,* Step 7.
[21] Spurgeon, C. H. "The Whole Machinery of Salvation," a sermon preached August 18, 1889. http://www.spurgeon.org, accessed December 17, 2013.
[22] Spurgeon, C. H. *The SoulWinner,* 180.
[23] Ibid.
[24] Little, Paul. *How to Give Away Your Faith.* (Downers Grove, Ill.: InterVarsity Press, 1973), 57–58.
[25] Spurgeon, C. H. "Soul Saving Our One Business." Sermon delivered Metropolitan Tabernacle.

[26] Scarborough, L. R. *With Christ After the Lost.* Southwestern Library of Centennial Classics, revised by E. D. Head, 1942.

[27] Exell, J. S. *The Biblical Illustrator: St. John* (Vol. 1). (London: James Nisbet & Co., n.d.), 250.

[28] Exell, J. S. *The Biblical Illustrator: Second Timothy–Titus, Philemon* (Vol. 2). (New York; Chicago; Toronto; London; Edinburgh: Fleming H. Revell Company. n.d.), 186.

[29] Whitesell, Faris. *Basic New Testament Evangelism.* (Grand Rapids: Zondervan Publishing House, 1949), 59.

[30] Criswell, W. A., P. Patterson, E. R. Clendenen, D. L. Akin, M. Chamberlin, D. K. Patterson & J. Pogue, (Eds.). *Believer's Study Bible* (electronic ed.). (Nashville: Thomas Nelson, 1991), Acts 16:31.

[31] Spurgeon, C. H. "The Christian's Great Business." Sermon delivered September 7, 1873, Metropolitan Tabernacle.

[32] Scarborough, L. R. *With Christ After the Lost*, 12.

[33] Spurgeon, C. H. "The Christian's Great Business." Sermon delivered September 7, 1873, Metropolitan Tabernacle.

[34] Spurgeon, C. H. "Retreat Impossible." Sermon delivered Metropolitan Tabernacle.

[35] Spurgeon, C. H. *The Soulwinner.*

[36] Beasley-Murray, G. R. *John* (Vol. 36). (Dallas: Word, Incorporated, 1999), 272.

[37] Robertson, Frederick W. "God's Revelation of Heaven," sermon delivered April 29, 1849.

[38] Hutson, Curtis. *Great Preaching on Soulwinning.* (Murfreesboro, TN: Sword of the Lord Publishers, 1989), 64.

[39] Scarborough, L. R. *With Christ After the Lost.*

[40] Sproul, R. C. "The New Genesis: The Holy Spirit and Regeneration." www.the-highway.com/genesis_Sproul.html, accessed May 21, 2010.

[41] Spurgeon. *The SoulWinner,* 277.

[42] Zodhiates, S. *The Complete Word Study Dictionary: New Testament* (electronic ed.). (Chattanooga, TN: AMG Publishers, 2000).

[43] Henry, M. *Matthew Henry's Commentary on the Whole Bible: Complete and Unabridged in One Volume.* (Peabody: Hendrickson, 1994), 1626.

[44] Leavell, Roland Q. *Evangelism: Christ's Imperative Commission,* 193.

[45] Dixon, Francis. "Bible Study No. 4: The Most Worthwhile Work in the World," June 27, 1967.

[46] Partly cited in Day, Richard Ellsworth. *The Shadow of the Broad Brim.* (Philadelphia: Judson, 1943), 131.

[47] Scarborough, L. R. *A Search for Souls.* (Nashville: The Sunday School Board of the Southern Baptist Convention, 1925), 15.

[48] Pink, A.W. *An Exposition of Hebrews: The Pinnacle of Faith,* Chapter 80, Hebrews 11:35–36.

[49] Bounds, E. M. *Power Through Prayer.*

[50] Rice, John R. *The Soulwinner's Fire.* (Murfreesboro: Sword of the Lord, 1941), 11.

[51] Smith, Bailey. *Real Evangelism,* 83.

[52] Spurgeon, Charles; T. De Witt Talmage; Henry Ward Beecher; D. L. Moody; Joseph Parker. *Gems of Truth & Beauty.* (Gideon House Books, 2017), 192.
[53] Taken from Whitesell, Faris Daniel. *Great Personal Workers.* (Chicago: Moody Press, 1956).
[54] https://www.preceptaustin.org/prayer_quotes, accessed June 15, 2022.
[55] Sanders, J. Oswald. *The Divine Art of Soul Winning,* 40–41.
[56] Spurgeon, C. H. "To Sunday School Teachers and Other Soul Winners," Sermon delivered October 19, 1873, Metropolitan Tabernacle.
[57] Spurgeon, C. H. *The Soulwinner.* (New Kensington: Whitaker House, 1995), 266.
[58] Spurgeon, C. H. *The Soulwinner,* Soulwinning Explained.
[59] Ibid., 168.
[60] Matthews, C. E. *Every Christian's Job.* (Nashville: Broadman Press, 1951), 1.
[61] Spurgeon, *The SoulWinner,* 271.
[62] Ironside, H. A. *Notes on the Book of Proverbs.* (Neptune, NJ: Loizeaux Bros., 1908), 129.
[63] Dixon, Francis. "Francis Dixon Bible Studies." *Getting on with the Job,* March, 1974.
[64] Brengle, S. L. *The Soul-Winner's Secret.* (Atlanta, Ga., 1948), Chapter 7.
[65] Finney, Charles. "The Divine Art of Soulwinning." www.believersweb.org/view.cfm?id=430&rc=1&list=multi-. Accessed April 12, 2010.
[66] Autrey, *Basic Evangelism,* 85.
[67] Matthews, C. E. *Every Christian's Job,* 57.
[68] Mullins, E. Y. *Talks on Soul Winning.* (Nashville, TN: The Sunday School Board of the Southern Baptist Convention, 1920), 14.
[69] *How to Lead a Soul to Christ,* (Zondervan).
[70] Whitesell, Faris. *Basic New Testament Evangelism,* 82.
[71] Leavell, Roland Q. *Winning Others to Christ,* 67.
[72] Mullins, E. Y. *Talks on Soul Winning.* (Nashville, TN: The Sunday School Board of the Southern Baptist Convention, 1920), 13.
[73] Spurgeon, C. H. *Morning and Evening,* October 8.
[74] Turnbull, Ralph G. (Ed.). *Evangelism Now.* (Grand Rapids: Baker Book House, 1972), 97–98.
[75] Spurgeon, C. H. *The Soul Winner.* (Whitaker House, 1995), 158.
[76] MacArthur, J. F., Jr. *Romans* (Vol. 1). (Chicago: Moody Press, 1991), 207.
[77] Fisher, Fred L. *Christianity Is Personal.* (Nashville: Broadman Press, 1951), 55.
[78] Autrey, C. E. *Basic Evangelism.* (Grand Rapids, Mich.: Zondervan Publishing House, 1968), 25.
[79] Toussaint, S. D. *Acts.* In J. F. Walvoord & R. B. Zuck (Eds.). *The Bible Knowledge Commentary: An Exposition of the Scriptures* (Vol. 2). (Wheaton, Ill.: Victor Books. 1985), 413.
[80] *Redemption—Accomplished and Applied,* 113.
[81] Criswell, W. A., P. Patterson, E. R. Clendenen, D. L. Akin, M. Chamberlin, D. K. Patterson, & J. Pogue (Eds.). *Believer's Study Bible* (electronic ed.). (Nashville: Thomas Nelson, 1991), Acts 16:31.

[82] Spurgeon, C. H. *The Soul Winner.* (Whitaker House), 29.

[83] Lifeway Research.

[84] Leavell, Roland Q. *Winning Others to Christ,* 39.

[85] Rogers, Adrian. *Adrianians.* (Memphis: Love Worth Finding Ministries, 2006), 175.

[86] *C. H. Spurgeon's Autobiography,* The Great Change—Conversion.

[87] The author was introduced to the tract ladder in 1975. Source unknown.

[88] www.biblebelievers.com/fuchida1.html. accessed March 12, 2010.

[89] Latourette, Kenneth Scott. *These Sought a Country,* 64.

[90] Spurgeon. *The Soul Winner,* 142.

[91] Ibid., 172–173.

[92] Leavell. *Winning Others to Christ,* 94–95.

[93] Spurgeon. *Spurgeon's Sermons on Soulwinning,* 17.

[94] Johnston, Thomas P. *Evangelizology.* (Liberty, Mo: Evangelism Unlimited, 2014), 1107.

[95] Whitney, Donald S. *Spiritual Disciplines for the Christian Life.* (Colorado Springs: NavPress, 1991), 111.

[96] Adeney, W. F. *The Pulpit Commentary.* "The Great Commission," Matthew 28:18–20.

[97] Henry, M. *Matthew Henry's Commentary on the Whole Bible: Complete and Unabridged in One Volume.* (Peabody: Hendrickson. 1994), 1776.

[98] Exell, J. S. *The Biblical Illustrator: Matthew.* (Grand Rapids, MI: Baker Book House, 1952), 687.

[99] Henry, M. *Matthew Henry's Commentary on the Whole Bible: Complete and Unabridged in One Volume.* (Peabody: Hendrickson. 1994), 2063–2064.

[100] Criswell, W. A., P. Patterson, E. R. Clendenen, D. L. Akin, M. Chamberlin, D. K. Patterson, & J. Pogue (Eds.). *Believer's Study Bible* (electronic ed.). (Nashville: Thomas Nelson, 1991), Ps. 126:6.

[101] Spurgeon, C. H. *The Treasury of David*: Psalms 120–150 (Vol. 6). (London; Edinburgh; New York: Marshall Brothers, n.d.), 70–71.

[102] Spurgeon, C. H. "Tearful Sowing and Joyful Reaping." Sermon delivered April 25, 1869, Metropolitan Tabernacle.

[103] Spence-Jones, H. D. M. (Ed.). *Psalms* (Vol. 3). (London; New York: Funk & Wagnalls Company, 1909), 223.

[104] Spurgeon, C. H. "Tearful Sowing and Joyful Reaping." Sermon delivered April 25, 1869, Metropolitan Tabernacle.

[105] Packer, J. I. *The J. I. Packer Classic Collection.* (Colorado Springs: NavPress, 2010), 170.

[106] Spurgeon, C. H. "The Christian's Great Business." Sermon delivered September 7, 1873, Metropolitan Tabernacle.

[107] Evans, William. *Instructions to the Soul Winner.* (Chicago: The Bible Institute Colportage Association, 1910).

[108] Mullins, E. Y. *Talks on Soul Winning.* (Nashville, TN: The Sunday School Board of the Southern Baptist Convention, 1920), 40.

[109] Ibid., 41.

110 Pinnock, Clark H. Set Forth Your Case. (Nutley, NJ: Craig, 1968), 88. (Bracket added by author for clarification.)

111 Garland, D. E. *2 Corinthians* (Vol. 29). (Nashville: Broadman & Holman Publishers, 1999), 271.

112 Spurgeon, *The SoulWinner,* 163.

113 *Vine's Dictionary of New Testament Words.*

114 Matthews, C. E. *Every Christian's Job.* (Nashville: Broadman Press, 1951), 20.

115 Garland, D. E. *2 Corinthians* (Vol. 29). (Nashville: Broadman & Holman Publishers, 1999), 270.

116 Exell, J. S. *The Biblical Illustrator: Second Corinthians.* (New York; Chicago; Toronto: Fleming H. Revell Company), 260.

117 Little, Paul. cited by www.defendingyourfaith.org/Apologetics.htm, accessed May 20, 2011.

118 Spurgeon, C. H. "Loving Persuasion." Sermon delivered at Metropolitan Tabernacle, June 26, 1887.

119 Exell, J. S. *The Biblical Illustrator: Second Corinthians.* (New York; Chicago; Toronto: Fleming H. Revell Company), 261.

120 Hutson, Curtis. *Great Preaching on Hell.* (Murfreesboro: Sword of the Lord Publishers, 1989), preface.

121 Ibid.

122 Spurgeon, C. H. "Loving Persuasion." Sermon delivered at Metropolitan Tabernacle, June 26, 1887.

123 Spurgeon, C. H. "Future Punishment a Fearful Thing." Sermon delivered March 25, 1866, Metropolitan Tabernacle.

124 Ruskin, John. "The Stones of Venice: The Fall." (Cosimo, Inc., 2013), 105.

125 Spurgeon, C. H. "A Preacher from the Dead." Sermon delivered July 26, 1857, at the Music Hall, Surrey Gardens.

126 Taken from: Whitesell, Faris Daniel. *Great Personal Workers.* (Moody Bible Institute of Chicago: Moody Press, 1956).

127 Autrey, C. E. *You Can Win Souls.* (Nashville: Broadman Press, 1961), 41.

128 Sanny, Lorne C.

129 *Evangelism Explosion.*

130 Smith, Jack, Ed. *Fifty Great Soul-Winning Motivational Sermons,* 19.

131 From *The Life and Sayings of Sam P. Jones: A Minister of the Gospel by His Wife,* 2nd and rev. ed. (Atlanta: Franklin-Turner Co., 1907).

132 Spurgeon, C. H. "The Two Effects of the Gospel." Delivered May 27, 1855, at Exeter Hall.

133 Chambers, Oswald. *My Utmost for His Highest,* May 5.

134 "Inspiring Quotes to Live By." www.soulwinning.info/gs/quotes.htm, accessed May 31, 2010.

135 Mullins, E. Y. *Talks on Soul Winning.* (Nashville, TN: The Sunday School Board of the Southern Baptist Convention, 1920), 9.

136 Autry, 27.

137 Leavell, Roland Q. *Winning Others to Christ,* 166.

[138] Murray, Andrew. *Working for God.* (New York, Chicago, Toronto: Fleming H. Revell, August 1901), Chapter 28.

[139] Leavell, Roland Q. *Winning Others to Christ*, 31.

[140] Torrey, R. A. *Personal Work,* 136.

[141] Spurgeon, C. H. "The Ethiopian." Sermon delivered May 15, 1884, Metropolitan Tabernacle.

[142] Scarborough, L. R. *With Christ After the Lost.* (Nashville: Broadman Press, 1952), 225–227.

[143] Mcduff, John Ross. *Sunsets on the Hebrew Mountains.* (New York: Robert Carter and Brothers,1862), 201.

[144] Riggs, Charles. *A Preliminary Look at Counselor Training, Amsterdam '83.*

[145] Scarborough, L. R. *With Christ After the Lost.* (Nashville: Broadman Press, 1952), 107–108.

[146] Graves, Stephen, Thomas Addington, Sean Womack. *The Mentoring Blueprint.* (Nashville: Word Publishing, 2000), 2.

[147] Mullins, E. Y. *Talks on Soul Winning.* (Nashville, TN: The Sunday School Board of the Southern Baptist Convention, 1920), 42.

[148] Henry, M. *Matthew Henry's Commentary on the Whole Bible: Complete and Unabridged in One Volume.* (Peabody: Hendrickson, 1994), 1664.

[149] Spurgeon, C. H. "Spring in the Heart." Sermon delivered February 11, 1866, Metropolitan Tabernacle.

[150] Downey, Murray. *The Art of Soulwinning.* (Grand Rapids, MI: Baker Book House, 1957), vi.

[151] Chambers, Oswald. *My Utmost for His Highest,* June 28.

[152] Gage, Freddie. "My Approach to Personal Soul-Winning," sermon taken from Jack Smith, Compiler. *Fifty Great Soul-Winning Motivational Sermons.* (Home Mission Board, 1994).

[153] Ellis, W. W. *We Are Witnesses.* (Kansas City: Beacon Hill Press, 1956), 92.

[154] Dobbins, G. S. *A Winning Witness,* 88.

[155] Sweazey, George. *Effective Evangelism.* (New York: Harper & Row Publishers, 1953),122.

[156] Spurgeon, C. H. *The Soulwinner,* "How to Win Souls to Christ."

[157] Wesley, John. *The Sermons of John Wesley,* Sermon 35 "The Law Established Through Faith: Discourse One," http://wesley.nnu.edu, accessed March 30, 2014.

[158] http://defendingcontending.com, March 30, 2014.

[159] Spurgeon, C. H. sermon, "A Plain Man's Sermon" (#1879).

[160] Spurgeon, C. H. *Spurgeon's Sermons on Soulwinning.* (Grand Rapid, MI: Kregel, 1995), 25.

[161] Bright, Bill. *The Christian and Witnessing: Bringing Words of Hope to the World Around You.* (New Life Publications, 1994), Step 7.

[162] Knight, Walter B. *Knights Illustrations for Today.* (Chicago: Moody, 1970), 320.

[163] Whitesell, Faris Daniel. *Great Personal Workers.* (Chicago: Moody Press, 1956).

<sup>164</sup> Torrey, R. A. *How to Bring Men to Christ.* (New York: Fleming. H. Revell Company, 1910), 100.

<sup>165</sup> Sweazey, George. *Effective Evangelism.* (New York: Harper & Row, 1953), 25.

<sup>166</sup> Scarborough. *With Christ After the Lost,* 154.

<sup>167</sup> Matthews, C. E. *Every Christian's Job,* 42.

<sup>168</sup> Dobbins, G. S. *A Winning Witness,* 84.

<sup>169</sup> Ibid.

<sup>170</sup> Trumbull, Charles. *Taking Men Alive.* (London: The Religious Tract Society, 1908), 37.

<sup>171</sup> Exell, J. S. *The Biblical Illustrator: Matthew.* (Grand Rapids, MI: Baker Book House, 1952), 41.

<sup>172</sup> Sweazey, George. *Effective Evangelism.* (New York: Harper & Row, 1953), 41.

<sup>173</sup> Courson, J. *Jon Courson's Application Commentary.* (Nashville, TN: Thomas Nelson, 2003), 42.

<sup>174</sup> Scarborough, L. R. cited in Faris Daniel Whitesell. *Great Personal Workers.* (Moody Press: Moody Bible Institute, 1956).

<sup>175</sup> Spurgeon, C. H. *The SoulWinner.* (Whitaker House, 1995), 53–54.

<sup>176</sup> Ibid., 11.

<sup>177</sup> Ibid., 36.

<sup>178</sup> Whitesell, Faris. *Basic New Testament Evangelism.* (Grand Rapids: Zondervan Publishing House, 1949), 181.

<sup>179</sup> Spurgeon, C. H. *An All-Round Ministry.* "How To Meet the Evils of the Age," Chapter 4.

<sup>180</sup> Whitsell, 114.

<sup>181</sup> Henry, M. *Matthew Henry's Commentary on the Whole Bible: Complete and Unabridged in One Volume.* (Peabody: Hendrickson, 1994), 979.

<sup>182</sup> Hutson, Curtis, (Ed.). *Great Preaching on Soul Winning.* (Murfreesboro, TN: Sword of the Lord Publishers), 234.

<sup>183</sup> Knight, Walter B. *Knight's Master Book of New Illustrations.* (Grand Rapids: Wm. B. Eerdmans, 1956), 644.

<sup>184</sup> National Association of Evangelicals (NAE)

<sup>185</sup> From "Wisdom on the Church."

<sup>186</sup> The points about the why of labor shortage influenced (adapted) by Lee Roberson's sermon "Labor Trouble."

<sup>187</sup> Smith, Bailey. *Real Evangelism.* (Nashville: Broadman Press, 1978), 85.

<sup>188</sup> Ibid.

<sup>189</sup> *Metropolitan Tabernacle Pulpit,* Sermon 1127.

<sup>190</sup> Towns, Elmer. *Winning the Winnable.* (Lynchburg, Va.: Church Leadership Institute, 1986), 6.

<sup>191</sup> Henry, M. and T. Scott. *Matthew Henry's Concise Commentary.* (Oak Harbor, WA: Logos Research Systems, 1997), Mt. 10:16.

<sup>192</sup> Morris, L. *The Gospel According to Matthew.* (Grand Rapids, MI; Leicester, England: W. B. Eerdmans; Inter-Varsity Press, 1992), 152.

<sup>193</sup> Blomberg, C. *Matthew* (Vol. 22). (Nashville: Broadman & Holman Publishers, 1992), 176.

[194] Rogers, Adrian. "The Sin of Silence" (sermon). http://www.sermonsearch.com, accessed December 1, 2013.

[195] Autrey, C. E. *Basic Evangelism.*

[196] Scarborough, L. R. *A Search for Souls.* (Nashville: Sunday School Board, 1925), 118.

[197] Leavell, Roland Q. *Winning Others to Christ,* 110–111.

[198] christianquotes.org/tag/cat/10/10. Accessed June 21, 2010.

[199] Spurgeon, C. H. *The Soul Winner.*

[200] Smith, Bailey. *Real Evangelism,* 118.

[201] Spurgeon, C. H. *Spurgeon's Sermons on Soulwinning.* (Grand Rapids: Kregel Publications, 1995), 9–10.

[202] Ogilvie, L. J. *The Preacher's Commentary Series* (Volume 28: Acts). (Nashville, Tennessee: Thomas Nelson Inc., 1983), 39–40.

[203] Blackaby, Henry. *Experiencing God.* (Nashville: B & H Publishers, 2008), 69.

[204] Wiersbe, Warren. *Classic Sermons on World Evangelism.* (Grand Rapids: Kregel Publications, 1999), 44–46.

[205] Zodhiates, S. *The Complete Word Study Dictionary: New Testament* (electronic ed.). (Chattanooga, TN: AMG Publishers, 2000).

[206] Spurgeon, C. H.

[207] Vassar, Thomas E. *Uncle John Vassar; or The Fight of Faith.* (Philadelphia: The Judson Press, 1879), 41.

[208] Spurgeon, C. H. "The Loving Persuasion." Sermon delivered June 26, 1887, Metropolitan Tabernacle.

[209] Adapted. www.sermonillustrator.org/illustrator/sermon3a/is_this_a_sign.htm.

[210] Spurgeon. *The Soul Winner,* "How to Induce Our People to Win Souls."

[211] Henry, M. *Matthew Henry's Commentary on the Whole Bible: Complete and Unabridged in One Volume.* (Peabody: Hendrickson, 1994), 1976.

[212] Exell, J. S. *The Biblical Illustrator: St. John* (Vol. 2). (London: James Nisbet & Co., n.d.), 119.

[213] Havner, Vance. *The Treasury of Vance Havner.*

[214] Murray, Andrew. *Working for God.* (New York, Chicago, Toronto: Fleming H. Revell, August 1901), Chapter 3.

[215] Spurgeon, C. H. "Tearful Sowing and Joyful Reaping." Sermon delivered April 25, 1869, Metropolitan Tabernacle.

[216] Sumner, Robert L. *Biblical Evangelism in Action,* 39.

[217] Spurgeon, C. H. *The Sword and the Trowel,* September 1878.

[218] Morgan, R. J. *Nelson's Annual Preacher's Sourcebook: 2002 Edition* (electronic ed.) (Nashville: Thomas Nelson Publishers, 2001), 40.

[219] Comfort, Ray. "Tips for Witnessing," September 9, 2021. https://livingwaters.com/tips-for-witnessing/, accessed August 5, 2023.

[220] Leavell, Roland Q. *Winning Others to Christ,* 106–107.

[221] Spurgeon. *The Soul Winner.*

[222] Elmer Towns.

223 Kemp, Joseph W. *The Soulwinner and Soulwinning.* (New York: Geroge H. Doran Company, 1916), 52. www.archive.org/stream/MN41613ucmf.../MN41613ucmf_8_djvu.txt. accessed April 13, 2010.
224 Bright, Bill. (Ed.). *Ten Basic Steps Toward Christian Maturity: Teacher's Manual.* (San Bernardino, California: Campus for Christ International, 1965), 352.
225 Autrey. *Basic Evangelism,* 87.
226 Jowett, John H. *Brooks by the Traveller's Way.* (New York: A. C. Armstrong & Son, 1902), 155–156.
227 Trumbull, Charles G. *Taking Men Alive.* (1907). www.navpress.com/magazines/archives/article, accessed May 23, 2010.
228 Simpson, Michael L. *Permission Evangelism,* 93–94.
229 Leavell, Roland Q. *Winning Others to Christ,* 93–94.
230 Torrey, R. A. *Personal Work,* 44.
231 Havner, Vance. *Pepper 'N Salt,* 59.
232 Spurgeon, C. H. *The Soul Winner.* (New Kensington, PA: Whitaker House, 1995), 20.
233 Trumbull, Charles. *Taking Men Alive.* (London: The Religious Tract Society, 1908), 70.
234 *Nelson's Annual Preacher's Sourcebook.* (Nashville: Thomas Nelson Publishers, 2010),72.
235 McGee, J. V. *Thru the Bible Commentary* (Vol. 3), (electronic ed.). (Thomas Nelson, 1997), 766.
236 Matthews, C. E. *Every Christian's Job,* 67.
237 Torrey, R. A. *Personal Work,* 25.
238 Spurgeon, C. H. "Spring in the Heart." Sermon delivered February 11, 1866, Metropolitan Tabernacle.
239 Berry, R. L. *The Soul-Winners Guide.* (James L. Fleming, 2005).
240 Exell, J. S. *Isaiah* (Vol. 3). (New York; Chicago; Toronto; London; Edinburgh: Fleming H. Revell Company, n.d.), 60.
241 Bridges, C. *An Exposition of the Book of Proverbs.* (New York: Robert Carter & Brothers, 1865), 143–144.
242 Scarborough, L. R. *A Search for Souls,* 65.
243 Henry, M. *Matthew Henry's Commentary on the Whole Bible: Complete and Unabridged in One Volume.* (Peabody: Hendrickson, 1994), 2077–2078.
244 Spurgeon, C. H. "The Christian's Great Business." Sermon delivered September 7, 1873, Metropolitan Tabernacle.
245 Lee, R. G. *Sermonic Library: From Feet to Fathoms.* (Orlando, Florida: Christ for the World Publishers, 1981), 52–55.
245 Ironside, H. A. *Notes on the Book of Proverbs,* 195.
246 Spurgeon, C. H. "Tearful Sowing and Joyful Reaping." Sermon delivered April 25, 1869, Metropolitan Tabernacle.
247 Sweazey, George. *Effective Evangelism.* (New York: Harper & Row Publishers, 1953), 64.

[248] Spurgeon, C. H. "Tearful Sowing and Joyful Reaping." Sermon delivered April 25, 1869, Metropolitan Tabernacle.

[249] *Sword of the Lord.* (July 25, 2008), 20.

[250] Rice, John R. *Personal Soulwinning.*

[251] Ryle, J. C. *The Upper Room,* 209.

[252] Autrey. *You Can Win Souls,* 23.

[253] Day, Richard. *The Shadow of the Broad Brim*, 156.

[254] Spurgeon, C. H. *Spurgeon's Sermons* (Vol. 8). (Grand Rapids: Baker Books, 1999), 233.

[255] Hallesby, Ole. *Prayer.* (Minneapolis, Minnesota: Augsburg Publishing House, 1931), 87–88.

[256] Spurgeon, C. H. *Autobiography,* Chapter XLV, 131.

[257] Spurgeon, C. H. "Tearful Sowing and Joyful Reaping." Sermon delivered April 25, 1869, Metropolitan Tabernacle.

[258] Spurgeon, C. H. "Soul Winning." Sermon delivered 1869, Metropolitan Tabernacle.

[259] Ibid.

[260] Downey, Murray. *The Art of Soulwinning,* 81.

[261] Spurgeon. *The SoulWinner,* back cover.

[262] Ibid., "Soulwinning Explained."

[263] Spurgeon. "Soul Winning," sermon delivered, 1869.

[264] Morgan, R. J. *Nelson's Annual Preacher's Sourcebook: 2002 Edition* (electronic ed.) (Nashville: Thomas Nelson Publishers, 2001), 40.

[265] Sanderson, Leonard. *Personal Soul Winning.* (Nashville: Convention Press, 1958), 7–8.

[266] Spurgeon, C. H. *The Soulwinner,* 189–190.

[267] Ibid., "The Soulwinner's Reward."

[268] Henry, M. *Matthew Henry's Commentary on the Whole Bible: Complete and Unabridged in One Volume.* (Peabody: Hendrickson, 1994), 1460.

[269] Spurgeon, C. H. "The Source." Sermon delivered July 6, 1876, Metropolitan Tabernacle.

[270] Mullins, E. Y. *Talks on Soul Winning.* (Nashville, TN: The Sunday School Board of the Southern Baptist Convention,1920), 11.

[271] *The Wisconsin Presbyterian,* August 12, 1912. (The Home Commission Committee of the Synod of Wisconsin), 9.

[272] Mullins, E. Y. *Talks on Soul Winning.* (Nashville, TN: The Sunday School Board of the Southern Baptist Convention,1920), 28.

[273] Leavell, Roland Q. *Evangelism, Christ's Imperative Command,* 4.

[274] Geisler, Norman. *The Big Book of Christian Apologetics.*

[275] Fitchett, W. H. *The Beliefs of Unbelief.* (New York: Jennings & Graham, 1907), 38.

[276] Chafer, Lewis Sperry. *Systematic Theology,* 8 vols. (Dallas: Dallas Seminary, 1947), 1:155, 157.

[277] Criswell, W. A. "The Reality of God," sermon delivered April 16, 1973, FBC, Dallas

[278] "Archaeology and the Bible." Christiananswers.net/archaeology, accessed December 27, 2010.

[279] Ibid.

[280] Ibid.

[281] Ibid.

[282] "Facing the Challenge." www.facingthechallenge.org, accessed December 22, 2010.

[283] McFarland, Alex. *10 Answers for Skeptics*, 49.

[284] MacArthur, John. "What Jesus' Death Meant to Him" (August 1, 1971). Gty.org, accessed June 14, 2011.

[285] Wilson, Larry. "Daily Devotional." January 23, 2011. www.opc.org/devotional.html?devotion, accessed June 17, 2011.

[286] Stanley, Charles. *Handbook for Christian Living,* 215.

[287] Pink, A. W. *Exposition of the Gospel of John.* (Bible Truth Depot, 1923–1945), 362.

[288] Torrance. *The Christian Doctrine of God.* (Edinburgh: T&T Clark, 1996), 51.

[289] Sproul, R. C., John Gerstner, and Arthur Lindsley. *Classical Apologetics,* 161.

[290] Geisler, Norman cited in Lee Strobel. *The Case for the Real Jesus*, 223.

[291] Criswell, W. A. *Criswell Study Bible,* 1 John 2: 2.

[292] Torrey, R. A. (Ed.). Fundamentals (Vol. IV), 319–320.

[293] Powell, Doug. *Resurrection Witness,* 14.

[294] Ibid.

[295] Doug Powell. The Resurrection Witness, 14.

[296] Licona, Michael cited in Lee Strobel. *The Case for the Real Jesus*, 122.

[297] Ibid.

[298] Hanegraaff, Hank. "The F-E-A-T that Demonstrates the FACT of Resurrection: Transformation." E-truth, April 18, 2014.

[299] Torrey, R. A. (Ed.). Fundamentals (Vol. IV), 319–320.

[300] https://www.communicatejesus.com/40-quotes-life-changing-power-resurrection/ accessed October 25, 2020.

[301] Spurgeon, C. H. "Perfect Sanctification." Sermon delivered in 1880, Metropolitan Tabernacle.

[302] Morgan, Christopher W., and Robert A. Peterson, (Ed.). Is Hell for Real or Does Everyone Go to Heaven? (Grand Rapids: Zondervan, 2004), 24–25.

[303] Spurgeon, C. H. "Future Punishment a Fearful Thing." Sermon delivered March 25, 1866, Metropolitan Tabernacle.

[304] Pink, A.W. "The Prison of Hell from Which There Is No Escape!"

[305] Lee, R. G. "Is Hell a Myth." Sermon contained in *Great Preaching on Hell.* Curtis Hutson, Ed. (Murfreesboro: Sword of the Lord Publishers, 1989), 91.

[306] Ryle, J. C. *Holiness.* (1816–1900).

[307] Ibid., 71–72.

[308] Ibid., 66.

[309] Ibid.

[310] Spurgeon, C. H. "Future Punishment a Fearful Thing." Sermon delivered March 25, 1866, Metropolitan Tabernacle.

[311] Munsey, Elbert. "The Awfulness of Eternal Punishment." Sermon in *Great Preaching on Hell*. Curtis Hutson, Ed. (Murfreesboro: Sword of the Lord Publishers, 1989), 155.

[312] Spurgeon, C. H. "Future Punishment a Fearful Thing." Sermon delivered March 25, 1866, Metropolitan Tabernacle.

[313] Ibid.

[314] Spurgeon, Charles H. *The Spurgeon Series 1859 & 1860: Unabridged Sermons in Modern Language.* (New Leaf Publishing Group, 2012), 1613,

[315] Exell, J. S. *The Biblical Illustrator: The Psalms* (Vol. 1). (New York; Chicago; Toronto: Fleming H. Revell Company), 476.

[316] Henry, M. *Matthew Henry's Commentary on the Whole Bible: Complete and Unabridged in One Volume.* (Peabody: Hendrickson, 1994), 986.

[317] Borchert, G. L. *John 12–21* (Vol. 25B). (Nashville: Broadman & Holman Publishers, 2002), 105.

[318] Barclay, W. (Ed.). *The Letters to the Galatians and Ephesians.* (Philadelphia, PA: The Westminster John Knox Press, 1976), 87.

[319] Henry, M. *Matthew Henry's Commentary on the Whole Bible: Complete and Unabridged in One Volume.* (Peabody: Hendrickson, 1994), 2284.

[320] Redpath, Alan. *Blessings Out of Buffeting.* (Grand Rapids: Fleming H. Revell, 1993), 78.

[321] Graham, Franklin with Donna Lee Toney. *Billy Graham in Quotes.* (Nashville: Thomas Nelson, 2011), 171.

[322] Criswell, W. A. *What to Do Until Jesus Comes Back.* (Nashville: Broadman Press, 1975), 20.

[323] Dixon, Francis. "Twelve Studies on the Life of Christ: The Certainty of His Return," No. 12 (August 24, 1974).

[324] Ibid.

[325] Criswell, W. A. *What to Do Until Jesus Comes Back.* (Nashville: Broadman Press, 1975), 20.

[326] MacArthur, J. F., Jr. *2 Peter and Jude.* (Chicago: Moody Publishers, 2005), 117.

[327] Curtis Hutson, Ed. *Great Preaching on the Second Coming.* (Murfreesboro, TN: Sword of the Lord Publishers, 1989), 16.

[328] Spurgeon, C. H. "Watching for Christ's Coming." Sermon delivered, April 7, 1889, Metropolitan Tabernacle.

[329] Criswell, W. A. *What to Do Until Jesus Comes Back.* (Nashville: Broadman Press, 1975), 17.

[330] Spurgeon, C. H. "Watching for Christ's Coming." Sermon delivered, April 7, 1889, Metropolitan Tabernacle.

[331] Spurgeon, C. H. "The Heaven of Heaven." Sermon delivered August 9, 1868, Metropolitan Tabernacle.

www.ingramcontent.com/pod-product-compliance
Lightning Source LLC
Chambersburg PA
CBHW070807100426
42742CB00012B/2280